Gien Karssen is a storyteller. Altho[ugh there are many] studies about the women in the B[ible, I have seldom found] one more practical than *Her Name Is Woman*. Gien makes these biblical women really come alive as you observe their actions and the effects of their lives. She helps you draw out applications that are relevant today. Gien is one of the best trainers I know for young Bible study leaders. She brings the Word of God to bear upon situations in day-to-day living. My prayer is that this book will work as a seed that brings forth much fruit.

CORRIE TEN BOOM
Author of *The Hiding Place*

All my life I have read about the women of the Bible, learning much from them even though they were somewhat vague, historic characters. In this book, these same characters have suddenly come alive. Because of Gien's careful research, sanctified imagination, and skill as a writer, I found myself understanding these women and their situations in a new way. Knowing more about the customs of their day helps us understand better why they acted as they did. It is interesting to note that God's women, down through the centuries, have enjoyed a freedom the world finds difficult to understand— the freedom to be and to do that which God intended. You will find this book both interesting and enlightening.

RUTH BELL GRAHAM
Author of *Footprints of a Pilgrim*

Believers

lessons from women of powerful faith

HER NAME IS WOMAN BIBLE STUDY

Gien Karssen

NavPress®

*A NavPress resource published in alliance
with Tyndale House Publishers, Inc.*

NAVPRESS

NavPress is the publishing ministry of The Navigators, an international Christian organization and leader in personal spiritual development. NavPress is committed to helping people grow spiritually and enjoy lives of meaning and hope through personal and group resources that are biblically rooted, culturally relevant, and highly practical.

For more information, visit www.NavPress.com.

Library of Congress Cataloging-in-Publication Data

Karssen, Gien.
   Her name is woman : believers : lessons from women of powerful faith / Gien Karssen.
      pages cm
      ISBN 978-1-63146-424-9
1. Women in the Bible—Biography.   2. Bible—Biography.   I. Title.
   BS575.K3693 2015
   220.9′2082—dc23   2015012056

Printed in the United States of America

21	20	19	18	17	16	15
7	6	5	4	3	2	1

I dedicate this book to my many friends within The Navigators organization around the world. The plan to write the Her Name Is Woman series began to ripen through my global contact with young women. I saw in them the same fascination for the lives of women in the Bible that I have.

I further remember many, many others, men and women, who through their teachings, example, and friendship have made an indelible impression upon my life. I think of the first Navigator I met years ago—Dawson Trotman, the founder of the organization—and of the many young people who have found a personal faith in Jesus Christ through the ministry of The Navigators recently.

They all have three things in common: a great love for God, a deep reverence for His Word, and a passion to share their lives with others. Two words are applicable to almost all of them: realism and enthusiasm.

Through my fellowship with The Navigators, the intense desire to be a woman after the heart of God grew within me. For this reason the women in this book are not just people of a dim, distant past, but real people, living and sparkling. It is my desire that every person who reads this book will be challenged in the same way to live wholeheartedly for God. It is my desire that they be encouraged and built up. And, at the same time, I trust this book will prove to be an instrument in their hands whereby they can help others.

Contents

Foreword

What do you want to be known for? When you come to the end of your days, what is it that you most hope your lasting legacy will be? Think on it a moment. Is not the answer that you were first and foremost a lover of God, and that you brought His love to all those you encountered?

So it is with the women you will soon learn more about. Their stories are not merely encouraging reminders of what is possible for us; their lives also shed the light of understanding upon our lives—and on the faithfulness of our good God.

These women are like us, living in a fallen world. There were many times for them when God felt far away, uninterested, or at best distracted. Continuing to believe that God is good and putting their faith into practice by seeking Him, praying, and worshiping Him in the midst of what seemed like silence on His part was hard. It is hard for me. It is hard for you, too. God knows that. He knows that our faith is often tested. He also knows that we come to know Him more deeply, believe Him more thoroughly, and love Him more wholeheartedly through the difficult times.

Over two thousand years ago, Jesus spoke the words "Don't be afraid; just believe" to the synagogue leader Jairus, and He is speaking them to us today. No matter what is going on around you or inside of you, Jesus says, "Look to Me. Walk with Me and keep on moving forward. Don't look at your fears or your failures; look at Me." He says, "All things are possible for those who believe."

Press on in your heart toward Him, dear sister. Be encouraged. God is faithful. His invitation is simply to *believe* Him and rest in His love. I know that is both the most difficult thing for us to do and the most vital. It may feel impossible to you some days, but nothing is impossible for God.

Just as these women knew.

Hebrews 11:6 says, "Without faith it is impossible to please God, because anyone who comes to him must *believe* that he exists and that he rewards those who earnestly seek him" (emphasis added). We are believers. We come to God because we believe He exists, we believe we need Him, and we believe that He is good. When we seek Him, the Bible promises, we will find Him—and finding Him is the most wonderful reward.

Jesus has done everything, paid everything, and won everything to win you. He believes you are priceless beyond measure. He invites us to believe Him, trust Him, and look to Him. For your everything. Even your legacy. He hasn't changed. The God of these women you are about to study has not changed. He has loved you from before the beginning of time.

Don't be afraid. Just believe.

Stasi Eldredge, author of Captivating *and* Becoming Myself

How to Use This Study

Do you long for a meaningful life? Do you want to become whole and fulfilled? These inborn, inner urges originate from the commission God gave woman at her creation. He expects woman, an equal partner with man, to be willing to step into her calling. The spiritual side of a woman is extremely important.

The women in this book are not fictional. They are real. They lived in history and, in their desires and problems, in their hopes and ambitions, are living among us today. Though the Bible doesn't share the full extent of their stories, I imaginatively explore what these women may have been doing and feeling in the time and place in which God placed them, in hopes that you will connect with their journeys even further.

As you learn about each of the women throughout the Her Name Is Woman series, the central question you must ask is, What place does God have in her life? The answer to this question decides the extent of every woman's happiness, usefulness, and motivation to keep moving forward. If God is absent, or if He is not given His rightful place, then life is without true purpose—without perspective.

As you read this book, join with these women of the Bible to consider your attitude toward God. And I hope that as you get acquainted with these women, you will make a fresh or renewed start in getting to know the Word of God.

I trust that meeting these women will turn out to be an unexpected gift for you and that you will resonate deeply with their experiences—and I pray that they will show you the way to a richer and happier life with God and other people.

AS YOU BEGIN

You may approach this book in one of two ways. First, just read it. The stories are intended to draw you deeply into the life of each woman in these pages. But be sure to include the Bible passages referenced at the beginning of each chapter in your reading. They are an important part of the book and are necessary for understanding the chapter. Second, you may wish to discuss the book in a small group. Considering the subjects and questions with some other people will add depth and greater insight to your study of these women.

Scripture references at the bottom of many pages will help you dig deeper into the Bible's wealth of truth and wisdom. You may answer the questions throughout each chapter personally or discuss them with your group. You may also conduct topical studies of these women or research accompanying themes. Whatever your direction might be, this study will become richer as you discuss these women with others, especially after your own individual preparation. Whether you do this study on your own or with others, be sure to use a journal so you may record your thoughts on the questions and any other things God impresses on your heart through the course of this study.

SUGGESTIONS FOR BIBLE STUDY GROUPS

1. Start with a small group—usually with a minimum of six and a maximum of ten people. This way your group will be large enough for an interesting discussion but small enough for each member to participate. As your numbers increase, start a second group.

2. Before you start the group, decide how often you want to meet. Many people may hesitate to give themselves to something new for an indefinite period of time. There are twelve chapters in each book of the Her Name Is Woman series, so they may easily be used as twelve-week studies. However, these books can just as easily work as six-week studies (two chapters per week). Some chapters are longer and will take more time to work through, while others are short enough to be combined into a two-part lesson. Please note that the number of questions varies depending on the length of the lesson. Discuss what process will work best for your group.

3. Remember that a Bible study group should discuss the Bible. While many of the questions within this book

are designed to help women examine their individual faith journeys, Scripture informs every piece of the study and should be referenced as an integral part of the discussion. Each participant should prepare her study at home beforehand so each member may share her personal findings.

4. Stress the necessity of applying the lessons learned, and help one another in doing this. There is a far greater need for spiritual growth than for an increase of knowledge. "How can what I learned influence my life?" is a question each participant should ask herself.

5. Determine, before you start, to attend every meeting. Miss only when you absolutely cannot attend. If you can't attend, do the study anyway and make up for it at the next meeting.

6. Consider yourself a member of the group. Feel free to make a contribution. Lack of experience should not keep you from taking part in the discussion. On the other hand, resist the temptation to dominate the group.

SUGGESTIONS FOR LEADERS OF BIBLE STUDY GROUPS

- Be sure that you have given sufficient time to your own Bible study and that you have completed it.
- Come prepared. Make notes of the points you want to stress.

- Begin and end on time. Set the tone by starting promptly at the first meeting.
- Few mountain climbers enjoy being carried to the top. Leave the joy of climbing to the group members. Don't do all the talking. Guide the discussion in such a way that each member of the group can participate.
- Don't allow any one person to dominate the conversation. Gently guide the group so each person may have an opportunity to speak. Sometimes it is necessary to talk privately with an overtalkative person, explaining the necessity of group participation. While some women may prefer to remain quiet, give them the opportunity to participate by asking them specific questions.
- Use the questions throughout each chapter as a jumping-off point, but feel the freedom to focus on issues that seem to particularly resonate with your group. However, don't allow the group to get too off topic. If a particular question becomes too time consuming or detracts from the overall study, redirect the conversation back to the main study. Getting back on track when the subject begins to wander can be done by saying, "Perhaps we could discuss this further after the study," or "Let's return to the main focus of the study."
- At the beginning of each session, open with prayer. Pray that Christ will speak to each person present by His Word. At the end of each session, pray for yourself and for each member of the group. Pray that the Holy Spirit will make you sensitive to the needs of others.

1

JOCHEBED

A Woman Who Traded Sorrow for Faith

When all kinds of trials and temptations crowd into your lives my brothers, don't resent them as intruders, but welcome them as friends! Realise that they come to test your faith.

JAMES 1:2-3, PH

READ

Exodus 1:8-22; Exodus 2:1-10

• • •

THE CRY OF A NEWBORN BABY cut through the reverent silence in the home.

Jochebed[1] sank into her pillows, tired. Briefly, a feeling of new motherly happiness flowed through her. She had once again brought a child into the world. Jehovah! His Name be praised! She had waited for this moment with great expectation, full of hope—and fear. "Is it a boy or a girl?" she asked anxiously.

Before the answer came, Jochebed was distracted by sounds

---

[1] Numbers 26:59

from outside. A whip cracked through the air and unmercifully cut the back of one of her fellow citizens. She heard a Hebrew screaming and the loud cursing of a furious Egyptian. Such sounds had become more familiar, as had the fear and tension that came with them. The situation of the Israelites in the Egyptian province of Goshen had been hard for a long time and was becoming increasingly worse.

As you begin this study, consider why the mother of Moses is listed in the ranks of the heroes of faith (Hebrews 11:23). What is faith, according to Hebrews 11:1?

Centuries before, the Egyptians had favored the Hebrews, largely due to the influence of Joseph, the son of Jacob. Through Joseph's insight and wise leadership, Egypt had withstood an immense famine, and the country became a haven for the entire Near East.[2] Years after Joseph died, the Egyptians continued to appreciate the Israelites.

Four centuries passed. God continued to bless His people in the foreign land—Israel's numbers increased, and her property holdings became larger and larger. But as God's blessing rested on Israel, the Egyptians began to feel threatened. They tightened their control over the Hebrews and tried to limit the Israelites' growth by suppression and forced

---

[2] Genesis 41:55-57, author's paraphrase

hard labor. Even those attempts failed. The Israelites began to multiply even faster.[3]

Finally Pharaoh tried to approach the problem at its roots and called for the two Hebrew midwives who helped the Israelite mothers with their deliveries. "Watch carefully whether a boy or a girl is born," he ordered, anger rising in his voice. "If it is a boy you must kill him, but let the girls live."[4]

That cruel order also failed to produce results, for the midwives showed more fear of God than of their king. They waved aside his orders with an excuse. "The Hebrew women have their babies so quickly that we cannot get there in time!" they said. "They are not slow like the Egyptian women."[5]

The situation had not changed three years later when this son of Amram and Jochebed was born.[6] Since the midwives refused to cooperate, the king now gave a new order, this time to the entire nation. "From now on," he decreed, "throw all Hebrew boys who are born into the Nile River."[7]

The order appalled the already pressured Israelites. For the Hebrew women, the joy of new motherhood turned into a dreadful tension. Their baby boys' first cries of life turned into death screams as their warm, little bodies were drowned in the chilly waters of the Nile. In horror the parents had to watch, over and over again, as crocodiles ate their newborn children.

"Crocodile food." Jochebed shuddered. "That is what Pharaoh makes of our flesh and blood." Then with a shock

---

[3] Exodus 1:7-14
[4] Exodus 1:16, author's paraphrase
[5] Exodus 1:19, author's paraphrase
[6] Referring to Aaron's birth three years earlier. See Exodus 7:7.
[7] Exodus 1:22, author's paraphrase

she came back to the reality of her own situation. Only a few seconds had passed since Jochebed had asked if the baby was a boy or girl. The midwife seemed hesitant to answer. When the woman finally looked at her, Jochebed saw fear in her eyes. "It is a boy," the midwife said with a sigh, compassion ringing through her voice.

"Give me the child," was all Jochebed could utter. A moment later she pressed the soft, pink little body to her heart. "What a beautiful child you are," she whispered. Then, as she looked her baby over from head to toe, a strange awareness came over her. This was not simply a beautiful baby; this child was in a special way related to God's plans. He was beautiful for God.[8]

God had plans for her little son. Jochebed could not define precisely what those plans would be, but she knew it for sure. From that moment on, she decided to fight for his life. The overtone within her heart would not be sorrow. She would trust in God.

When you are faced with sorrow and darkness, what is your response? The future can feel undefined and even hopeless at times. List three things we can learn from Jochebed about trust in the midst of these times.

Jochebed and her husband were Levites and thus belonged to the tribe that would later be assigned to serve God in His

[8] Acts 7:20

temple. Although both of them were born into slavery, they had kept their faith in God. Jochebed continually directed the antenna of her faith toward Him. Because of this faithfulness, she received His messages and gained inner convictions about things that would be revealed later.

What is faith? It is the confident assurance that something we hope for will happen. It is the certainty that what we hope for is waiting for us even though the possibility seems slim (Hebrews 11:1). All Christians have been justified by faith through Christ (Galatians 2:16), but in order to receive answers to their prayers, they must pray with faith (Matthew 21:22). If they doubt and do not pray with faith, however, their prayers will go unanswered, because whatever is done apart from faith is sin (Romans 14:23).

How have you seen the correlation between faith and conviction in your life? Give a specific example of a time when faith led to confidence in God's future work.

God was about to do something great for the world, for the suppressed Hebrews, and for this tested family. And, as He usually does in history, He drew a human being into His plan. Much would depend on Jochebed's faith and how much she was attuned to His leading.

In what ways can you be more attuned to God's leading? What things distract you from watching for His leading?

The Bible shows that God honored Jochebed and her husband. Their faith gave them the courage to ignore the king's command.[9] They obeyed a higher leadership: God. Against Pharaoh's expressed order, they hid their child day after day after day. Their motivation was obedience to God, as well as love for the child.

What did they expect? A miracle? That solution no doubt lay within the possibilities. God, who out of nothing created man and animals and the entire creation, had the power to do anything. His power was not shortened. Every possibility was available to Him.

Think of a recent (or current) trial you have gone through. As you considered how to get through it, what possible solutions came to mind? Was a miracle one of those solutions, or was it something you dismissed outright? How can we rest in the goodness of God regardless of outcomes?

9 Hebrews 11:23

Gradually Jochebed began to understand that God was going to work a miracle through her. Yet for the time being, everything remained the same. The atmosphere in the country continued to be oppressive and hostile against the Hebrews. The king had not relented. Every day it became more difficult to hide the baby from the outside world. His tiny voice became stronger, and his crying increasingly became a matter of concern.

Jochebed could not possibly imagine how fascinating God's orders were for this child uniquely called by Him. "Every child comes into the world with 'sealed orders.' Every human being has a unique destiny to fulfill."[10] That she daily bathed, clothed, and fed a child who would become one of the world's greatest national leaders was beyond her understanding. God had chosen her son to become one of the greatest personalities of the Old Testament. As a man, Moses would pass on God's laws to the Hebrew people, laws that centuries later would still be considered the foundation of society. He foreshadowed God's Son—the Messiah to come—and the stewardship of this future had been placed in the hands of his mother.

What miracles might God be working through you? What special stewardships has He placed in your hands?

---

10 Larry Christenson, *The Christian Family* (Minneapolis, MN: Bethany, 1970), 64.

The problems of God's people at this time in history seemed insurmountable, but God had no problems—only plans. And His plans would be announced through this child.

During the days that came and went, insecurity and faith fought for precedence in Jochebed's life. She dealt with human insecurities concerning the child, but she also had the assurance of faith. This testing period made Jochebed's faith grow and gave her courage.

Think of a specific time when insecurity and faith fought for precedence in your life. How did you respond? What did your relationship with God look like as you emerged from that time?

Her growing faith made her inventive. She became skilled in hiding the child and in developing ideas to spare his life. She learned how to educate little Aaron so that he wouldn't betray his baby brother. She modeled wisdom and faith for Miriam, her only daughter, despite all the details of taking care of the baby. God also had sealed orders for these two children, whose futures were closely connected with that of the baby. Jochebed was responsible for their development as well as for that of her baby son.

The plan that Jochebed developed was simple and close at hand. Though it was based on facts that she had carefully put together, this plan was above all inspired by faith. God Himself prompted the ideas in her mind.

First she transformed a simple box made of reeds—maybe her shopping basket—into a little boat. The woven papyrus reeds would protect the baby against crocodiles, who seemed to have little interest in eating reeds. Then she carefully coated the inside of the box with waterproof bitumen and tar.[11] The water that was threatening the tiny boy with death would instead save his life.

Calmly and carefully, Jochebed went to work. Every possibility was thought through. Gradually, as she developed her own good solutions, she fell in step with the plans God had formed in heaven for His servant on earth. Her part in His plan was vitally important, but she could only move in the directions He pointed out to her.

Do you view your actions as a vital part of God's plan for you? In what directions might He be pointing you right now that require you to step forward in faith?

Because of Jochebed's faith, problems didn't have a chance to develop. They didn't paralyze or isolate her. On the contrary, her trials paved the way to greater possibilities. Her difficulties became her friends instead of her enemies.

Jochebed made the salvation of her youngest child a family affair. Through her approach, the problems and concerns

---

[11] Exodus 2:3

became a blessing to the entire family. Her husband was one with her in her faith. Yet it was she, the mother, who especially put her seal on the members of the family during this difficult time and welded them together as instruments for God.

She had the courage to involve her young daughter in her plans. That also was a step of faith. When she placed the little boat in the waters of the Nile River, Jochebed took her hands off her son and placed him into the care of God. The future of her little boy now lay solely in His hands and those of little Miriam.

Miriam unobtrusively kept watch over the floating cradle, demonstrating how carefully she had been trained for this task.[12] The poise and trust of the mother characterized the daughter.

Faith replicates itself. Who in your life might be watching you closely, learning how to rest in the promises of God through your example? Does this inspire you to grow in faith?

When Pharaoh's daughter noticed the box and had it picked up out of the Nile, Miriam conducted herself in an exceptionally mature manner. As soon as she saw that her brother was safe with the princess, she stepped forward. No word or motion betrayed how personally she was related to this child. The sound of her voice was controlled. Her

---

[12] Exodus 2:4

behavior created no suspicion. "Shall I go and get one of the Hebrew women to nurse the baby for you?"[13] she asked.

"Yes, go,"[14] the princess answered, not knowing that with those words she gave the child back to his mother. So during a time of terrible persecution, Jochebed was able to care for her son openly without feeling threatened. She was even being paid to do so by the daughter of the man who had tried to kill her child. That was divine humor.

After the child had grown older and the princess had adopted him as her own son, she named him Moses. "That will be his name," she said, "because I have drawn him out of the water."[15]

Think through Jochebed's situation carefully and list all the "enemies" (whether people or difficult circumstances) she faced. Which of these "enemies" turned into "friends"? Do you have certain difficult circumstances in your life that God's power and grace could change into "friends"? If so, what are they?

Moses had been rescued; his future was completely secure. After the early years under his mother's care, he received the best opportunities in Pharaoh's court that any young man of his time could have wished for. He, the son of a Hebrew slave

---
[13] Exodus 2:7
[14] Exodus 2:8
[15] Exodus 2:10, author's paraphrase

family, received the education of a prince. All the possibilities of the mighty and learned Egyptians were at his disposal. And while Hebrew babies were still dying premature deaths, Moses was being prepared for the task for which God had chosen him. His sealed order was to become the redeemer of his people.

Jochebed continued to have a part in that preparation. The few years that Moses had been under her wings helped to determine his future. Her faith in God had become familiar to him. His people's complete commitment to God made an indelible impression on his receptive soul; the attractions of the heathen palace had little to offer him.

When Moses became a grown man, he preferred the sufferings of his people above the riches of Egypt. He developed into a man of faith[16] who walked daily with the unseen God as if he could see Him. He became a friend of God.[17] This was an exceptional compliment to be given to a human being.

---

*Like Moses, we are called God's friends
(John 15:15). And more than that, we are
His children (Galatians 3:26). How has
this knowledge impacted your life?*

Jochebed had received the meaning of her name: "Jehovah is her glory." Had that name been given to her by believing

---

[16] Hebrews 11:24-29
[17] Exodus 33:11

parents in the hope that she would work for God's glory in her life? Did she choose the name herself as a public witness of her deepest thoughts, or was it a name of honor granted to her by God?

The Bible mentions her name only twice,[18] but it is forever engraved in history as the name of one of the most important mothers who ever lived. Probably never in history have three children of one mother, Jochebed, ever had such an influence at the same time.

Her children demonstrated to the world the place that God had in their mother's heart. His honor had been her highest purpose. They also illustrated that principle with their own lives. When Moses was the leader of the Israelite nation,[19] Aaron was its high priest who symbolized God's holiness and grace toward His people.[20] As the high priest, he represented God to the people and the people to God. And as the intercessor for his people, he foreshadowed Christ.[21]

Miriam also played a part in the leadership of God's people, which for a woman was a rare exception in Israel's history. She was the nation's first prophetess and used her gifts in music and song to lead the Hebrew women into bringing honor to God.[22]

So Jochebed's three children used their lives in the service of God. Their mother had the laws of God in her heart long before she imprinted them in the hearts of her children as the

[18] Exodus 6:20; Numbers 26:59
[19] Micah 6:4; Psalm 106:23
[20] Exodus 28:1
[21] Hebrews 2:17; 5:1-5
[22] Exodus 15:20-21

Bible commands.[23] She accomplished her feats and ministries by believing the promises of God.

Consider Jochebed's life in light of Genesis 50:20 and Romans 8:28. Explain how these verses were true in Jochebed's life.

Jochebed lived far too early to be familiar with these words of James: "Consider it pure joy, my brothers and sisters, whenever you face trials of many kinds, because you know that the testing of your faith produces perseverance."[24] But she did experience the truth of his words, just like the other men and women—heroes of faith—in whose ranks she is listed. These people achieved unusual and great things because they believed in the almighty God.[25]

Despite often hostile environments, the people Scripture proclaims as heroes of faith thought vertically instead of horizontally, spiritually instead of according to their own human natures. Convinced that their God was greater than the greatest difficulty, they courageously faced immense problems. They experienced how much God desired to surprise them, and what a small thing it was for Him to change their sorrow into faith.

---

[23] Deuteronomy 6:6-7
[24] James 1:2-3
[25] Hebrews 11:1-40

2
HANNAH

A Woman Who Believed in Prayer

The great people of the earth today are the people who pray. I do not mean those who talk about prayer . . . nor yet those who can explain about prayer; but I mean these people who *take* time and *pray*. They have not time. It must be taken from something else. This something else is important. Very important, and pressing, but still less important and less pressing than prayer.

S. D. GORDON, *QUIET TALKS ON PRAYER*

READ

1 Samuel 1:1-28

• • •

HANNAH WAS WEIGHED DOWN with the misery of her marriage. Her husband loved her, but his other wife was cruel, mocking her for her lack of children. How had the difficulties in her marriage emerged? Had she, like Sarah, prompted her husband to take a concubine when he discovered that they wouldn't have children?[1] Had she been unable to resist Elkanah's love, becoming his second wife after he had already married Peninnah? Or had Elkanah, an otherwise God-fearing man, become a bigamist of his own

---
[1] Genesis 16:1-2

initiative, drawing Hannah into a situation entirely out of her control?

In any case, none of them had foreseen the far-reaching consequences of two marriages. It resulted in terrible misery for each of the three marriage partners.

---

*Read Judges 21:25 and 1 Samuel 2:11-36.
What was the situation of Hannah's
people, nationally and spiritually?*

But the Bible does say that Hannah was a woman who had definite access to God. The way to Him was open to her on the basis of forgiveness of sin by means of the sacrifices that her husband, as head of the family, regularly made to the Lord.

Sometimes someone is tested to the very roots of her being, and it seems as if some unseen power is operating to extinguish her life. Hannah must have felt that way. She had shed countless tears because she felt forsaken by God since she had no children.

Elkanah, wanting to comfort Hannah, had given her a double portion of sacrificial meat. Wasn't his love more to her than ten sons? She had been happy with this expression of his love, but these words had made her even more lonesome. Had Elkanah given up the hope of ever having a child by her?

Abraham, she remembered, had wrestled with God about a child.[2] Isaac, in a similar situation, had prayed for his wife.[3]

[2] Genesis 15:2-6
[3] Genesis 25:21

And their wives had given birth, even later in life, to sons who had come to mean so much to her people. Those sons had been part of God's plan for Israel.

God! He is the only One who understands me, the only One who can help me, she thought. She went back to the tabernacle, alone. There she broke down before God. Heartbroken, without words. At first she wasn't even able to voice her thoughts.

Then, when her heart had somewhat unburdened itself, her lips breathed a prayer, though her voice remained silent. "O LORD of hosts . . . ,"[4] she began. The way she spoke to Him declared her vision of Him. He was the Lord of the hosts of heaven and earth, of everything He had created.[5] An immense host of angels stood at His disposal.[6] He was the Lord who had performed many miracles for Israel as a nation.

Those four words, "O LORD of hosts," expressed her faith in His greatness and might.[7] *In light of His majesty, I am nothing*, she thought. *Only a servant, a handmaid.* She repeated this thought several times. The words were chosen carefully. She considered herself an insignificant earthly creature in the light of a holy God, yet she wanted to serve Him. This was a proper set of values, for she—though a lowly human being—could serve God.

Realizing this, Hannah presented God with a great petition. She did not insult Him by asking for a small favor. One

[4] 1 Samuel 1:11, ESV
[5] Genesis 2:1
[6] Genesis 32:1-2; Luke 2:13
[7] Commentator Matthew Henry says that this was the first time a person had addressed God in this manner.

doesn't ask for a few pennies from a multimillionaire. From such a great God one shouldn't expect anything short of a miracle—a real miracle.

Hannah didn't pray vaguely. She made a specific request: "God, I want to have a son." Her prayer was followed by a promise: "Then I will give him back to You for all of his life, and no razor will ever touch his head."[8] Her son, if God granted him, would be a Nazirite, a man dedicated to Him, who would drink no wine and who would never cut his hair.[9]

Compare Hannah's prayer carefully with the Lord's Prayer (Matthew 6:9-13). What resemblances do you see? How can this inform your own prayer life?

Was Hannah actually saying, "God, You know that I desire to have a child, but even more than asking this for myself, I ask this for You"? It is possible.

The religion of her people—that is, the religion of its priests—had lost its meaning. It had been corrupted. Yet Hannah had preserved her faith and kept it pure. However, her influence was limited. What the country needed was a man who could become a link between God and His people, who could bridge the gap and usher in a new future.

Did Hannah's heart cry out only for herself, or was she

---

[8] 1 Samuel 1:11
[9] Judges 13:3-5; Amos 2:12; Luke 1:15

also weeping for God and for her people? Was this why her prayer had such a far-reaching impact? Did she realize what part she could have in the spiritual solution of this national problem? It is possible, though the scriptural record is too brief to determine this.

Are there ways in which the Christian religion has become corrupted? How can you keep your faith pure in the midst of fallen humanity?

The decay of the people and the priesthood was also indicated by Eli's treatment of Hannah. He had little human understanding, little compassion.

"How long will you be drunk?" he lashed out at her. "Put away your wine."[10] The priest who hadn't dared deal harshly with his own sons felt no reservation in treating Hannah in such a way. The old man revealed a lack of insight and poor self-control.

His words also revealed that in those days, drunk people and bad women were not an unusual sight in the house of God. Even Eli's own sons slept with the women who gathered at the door of the tabernacle.[11]

Hannah, however, was in the presence of God and so felt no desire to defend or justify herself. She didn't express any shame or indignation but explained the situation in a few

---

[10] 1 Samuel 1:14, author's paraphrase
[11] 1 Samuel 2:22

words. Eli suddenly became what he should have been: the priest of God. As the representative of the Lord, he said, "Go in peace. The God of Israel will grant your petition."[12] He didn't know the nature of her request, but as instructed by God, he told her she had been heard.

With these words the peace of God that follows each faithful prayer came into her heart.[13] She had taken her cares to God and left them in His hands.

———————

What role does prayer play in your walk with the Lord? Do you experience peace by taking your petitions to Him, regardless of the outcome? If prayer is a minor part of your life, how can Hannah's example spur you on toward increased faith and a deeper relationship?

———————

"Now faith is the assurance of things hoped for, the conviction of things not seen," the author of Hebrews wrote many centuries later.[14] That was what Hannah experienced. The assurance that her prayer was heard entered her heart. Outwardly the change was remarkable—her appetite returned and her face no longer held any trace of sadness.[15] She lived her faith, trusting God in such a way that other people noticed.

[12] 1 Samuel 1:17, author's paraphrase
[13] Philippians 4:6-7
[14] Hebrews 11:1, ESV
[15] 1 Samuel 1:18

What strikes you most about Hannah's dedication to God?

Samuel, which means "heard by God," was born within a year. Then the meaning of Hannah's own name—"gracious" or "favor"—began to make sense. Instead of being a neglected woman, she had become an extraordinarily privileged one, for her prayer marked a turning point in history.

Do you view prayer as powerful enough to impact the future of nations? List some Scripture passages that speak more deeply of the power of prayer. Which one impacts you the most, and how might it transform how you pray?

It was not long before God's Word was again heard in all of Israel.[16] The Lord revealed Himself through Samuel even when Samuel was still a boy. From Dan, far to the north, to Beersheba, far to the south, the people acknowledged that Samuel was a prophet appointed by God.[17]

The people turned from idols to serve God. The ark of the Lord, which had been taken for spoil and dishonored by the Philistines, was returned.[18] The Philistines made peace with Israel, for the hand of the Lord was against the Philistines all the days of Samuel. Cities that had been lost in battle were regained.

---

[16] 1 Samuel 3:21–4:1
[17] 1 Samuel 3:19-20
[18] 1 Samuel 4:11; 6:1–7:1

The faith of Hannah lived in her son. Centuries later his name would be listed among the heroes of faith,[19] for he was one of the men who through faith had subdued kingdoms.

Samuel, who had been born in answer to prayer and whose name constantly reminded him of that, became a man of prayer himself. He felt it was a sin for people not to pray.[20] This attitude may have been the key to the many answers he received.

---

*Consider these words: "It is a sin not to pray."
How does this make you feel? Does it change your
perspective on the place of prayer in your life?*

Only eternity will reveal what Israel, whom Samuel served as a prophet, priest, and judge, and the millions who have since studied his life, owe to Samuel's life and ministry.

Oh, Hannah, were you not favored when you saw the results of the answer to your prayer? And were you not as privileged as Sarah and Rebekah to see your child playing such a role in history?

---

*Hannah's song of praise (1 Samuel 2:1-10)
reveals her deepest thoughts. What does
she think of God? Write your own song of
praise to God, using His work in your life
and in the world to inform your words.*

---

[19] Hebrews 11:32-33
[20] 1 Samuel 12:23

Mary, the mother of Christ, must have been influenced by Hannah's prayer and her touching song of praise when she offered her Magnificat.[21] Hannah had a wonderful time during the period in which her child grew from a baby to a toddler. It passed quickly, however. As soon as Samuel was weaned, she fulfilled her promise and gave him back to God. From then on, she saw him only once a year, when she and her husband offered their sacrifices at Shiloh.[22]

Her prayer was radical in nature. So was her dedication. She had to offer Samuel to God daily, trusting Him to protect Samuel's faith in the midst of the corruption he saw in Eli and his sons.

Prayer, faith, and dedication continued to characterize her life, for Hannah knew that a person who gave all to God would receive more in return. God will never be any person's debtor. He gave her five more children.[23]

What did Hannah receive in return for the son she dedicated to God? (Read 1 Samuel 2:21.) What does that teach us about the nature of God? Think of a time when God answered your prayer, even if it was not necessarily in the timing or way you would have chosen. How could knowing that His character never changes, regardless of circumstances, alter the way you pray?

---

[21] Luke 1:46-55
[22] 1 Samuel 1:24-28; 2:19
[23] 1 Samuel 2:21

Why could Hannah count on answered prayer? Because she had met God's prerequisites. These prerequisites were not neatly collected in a single passage of Scripture, but they were principles that, in her walk with God, she sensed and knew. These included

1. Praying because her sin was forgiven.[24]
2. Pleading in God's name, acknowledging His greatness.[25]
3. Being humbled by her own nothingness.[26]
4. Formulating a clear, well-defined petition.[27]
5. Desiring that God's will be done and His kingdom extended.[28]
6. Praying in faith.[29]

While these prerequisites do not mean that our prayers will be answered in the time and way we think they should be, they do open up the relational pathways as we connect with God: "If . . . My people who are called by My name humble themselves and pray and seek My face and turn from their wicked ways, then I will hear from heaven, will forgive their sin and will heal their land."[30] Call out to God, and be assured that He will hear you.

---

[24] Psalm 66:13-19
[25] John 16:24
[26] 2 Samuel 7:18-29
[27] Matthew 7:7-11
[28] Matthew 6:10
[29] Hebrews 11:6; Matthew 21:22
[30] 2 Chronicles 7:14, NASB

3

RAHAB

A Prostitute in the Gallery of the Heroes of Faith

An innkeeper's bill from Roman days:
Wine and bread, 1 ace.
Hot meal, 2 ace.
Hay for mule, 2 ace.
One girl, 8 ace.

THEODOR BIRT, *AUS DEM LEBEN DER ANTIKE*

READ

Joshua 2:1-21; Joshua 6:22-25

. . .

THE BIBLE IS AN HONEST BOOK that states facts as they are—candidly. Rahab, the Bible says, was a prostitute, a woman who sold her body for money.[1] People have tried to cover up this sad fact, stating that she was an innkeeper. This was probably also true, but the fact remains that she was a woman of corrupted morals.

In those days the innkeepers were women, never men. In the written bills of later Roman times, an amount was annotated for the meal and the girl, but the cost of the bed was

---

[1] Joshua 2:1

not mentioned—it apparently was included with the price of the girl. She provided an "extra service" by offering her body, and this was included in the bill.

Since Rahab was in a position to lodge guests, it was natural for Joshua's spies to go to her place. Jericho was a small town, and Rahab's inn was probably the only place to sleep.

Since Rahab was a prostitute in a small town, we can safely assume that she was an outcast. What are some other examples in the Bible of God using outcasts and people of low repute for His glory?

Did Rahab initially suspect that these foreigners—decent men without hidden motives—were Israelites? The Bible doesn't say. But it does say that counterespionage was launched immediately. The king heard that Jewish scouts were in the city and called for their immediate capture.[2]

Meanwhile, Rahab had become aware of the true identity of her guests and had already hidden them on her roof under stacks of flax.[3] Since it was harvest time and the walled city was small, the inhabitants of the tiny houses on the narrow streets had to use every available inch of space for storage. An open roof was the least ideal spot to hide people since others could see everything that went on there, even from

---

[2] Joshua 2:2,7
[3] Joshua 2:6

a distance. But Rahab's house was different. It was built on the double city wall[4] and was situated higher than any other house, so no curious eyes could watch what went on there. The spies would be safe, but only for a short time.

Rahab misled the king's messengers. While they searched the surrounding countryside carefully, she talked with the hidden spies.[5] She told them she was aware that God had given them the land and that the inhabitants of her land were fearful of them because of the miracle of the parting of the Red Sea.[6] She was well aware of what God had done for His people. She told them that the men had lost courage to face the Israelites because of their God.[7]

What strikes you about Rahab's knowledge of the God of Israel? Does your understanding of God inform your actions? In what ways could considering the power of God impact how you respond to situations?

She proved to be a wise woman who acted in the light of proper information. She used discretion in talking about the spies and shrewdness in hiding them. She felt that one good turn deserved another: "Since I have saved your lives, will you in turn save mine and that of my relatives?"[8]

---

[4] Joshua 2:15
[5] Joshua 2:4-5,7-13
[6] Exodus 14:26-30
[7] Joshua 2:11-12
[8] Joshua 2:12-13, author's paraphrase

She naturally expressed concern about herself while at the same time expressing faith in the God of Israel. She believed that He fought for His people and that He was going to give them this land. She also believed that because of this God's power, her people didn't have the slightest chance of keeping the Israelites outside the city walls. She acted upon this faith.

Rahab's faith served as the basis for her wise request. What are some examples of when wisdom has emerged from faith in your life?

She asked for a sign that they would save her when their armies returned to take the city. They told her that if she put a scarlet cord in her window, no one in her household would be harmed.[9]

Some Bible commentators say that this scarlet cord represented Rahab's immoral occupation. It was her "red light" and therefore would cause no suspicion. Nobody would suspect it to be a sign of espionage. This may or may not have been the case, but it was certainly a clear indication of an agreement between the two parties.

Rahab did not delay. The men had hardly left when she bound the red cord at her window.[10] She wanted to be absolutely certain that her house was easily distinguishable from all the others.

God likes it when people—even unbelievers—take their

[9] Joshua 2:12-13,17-18
[10] Joshua 2:21

business seriously. Jesus proved this later when He told His disciples that the sons of this world are wiser in their own generation than the sons of light.[11]

Read the parable of the shrewd manager in Luke 16. Pay close attention to verse 10. How do the principles in that parable parallel Rahab's actions?

A week later, the miracle of the Red Sea repeated itself. Again deep water was parted. The Israelites walked with dry feet through the river Jordan, which at that time was high above its banks.[12] A few days later, Rahab saw a throng of Israelites walking around the city in silent procession. The city gates were closed. No Jew could come in; no Canaanite could get out. This state of affairs continued for six days.[13]

Now and then Rahab reassured herself that the red cord was definitely visible. Her life would soon depend upon its being seen.

On the seventh day, the Israelites again walked around and around the city.[14] Their faces were solemn. The tension on both sides of the wall was becoming unbearable. Inside, the people viewed the future with eyes full of horror and fear—except in one house. In Rahab's home there was hope and trust. She had made a covenant with the people of God and, therefore, with God Himself.

---

[11] Luke 16:8
[12] Joshua 3:15-17
[13] Joshua 6:1-3
[14] Joshua 6:4

---

*Read James 2:14-25, focusing particularly
on the reference to Rahab in verse 25.
How is Rahab's story a good illustration
of the true faith James is talking about?*

Seven priests each blew a trumpet made from a ram's horn, and the army, at Joshua's command, began to shout. Then the unbelievable happened. The earth began to tremble. Walls that had safeguarded the city for years crumbled and fell apart, leaving the city unprotected.[15]

The writer of Hebrews later said faith had caused the walls to fall. And that very same faith caused a part of the wall to remain intact—the wall where Rahab's house stood.[16]

---

*Why, according to Hebrews 11:31, didn't Rahab
perish with those who were disobedient?
What actions and attitudes proved her faith?*

Both parties had fulfilled their part of the agreement. Rahab had done her part, and God had rewarded her faith. Her faith in the victory of the God of Israel was so strong that she was able to convince her relatives to come and stay with her. Every one of them was spared.

---

[15] Joshua 6:20
[16] Hebrews 11:30-31

Rahab's faith had an enormous impact on her relatives. Have you considered what your example of faith could do in the lives of your family? Who in your family needs to see faith in action right now?

Rahab's life portrait was marred because of the dishonoring stain of immorality. Yet it was brightened by an example of glistening faith—faith strong enough for her to act. This was necessary, says James,[17] for if faith cannot stand the test of use, then it is useless—dead. Inner faith can only be recognized by outward deeds.

One definition of faith is that it is a fixed and profound trust in God and His Word. Rahab had this kind of faith. Therefore, God took her tarnished portrait, cleansed it, and hung it along with Sarah's in the gallery of the heroes of faith.[18]

Each of us had a tarnished portrait before we met Christ. How has God redeemed your past sin and cleansed you for His purposes? Praise Him for His work in your life.

Rahab, like Sarah, a heroine of faith? Yes. For God is no respecter of persons.[19] There are no impossible cases with

[17] James 2:17
[18] Hebrews 11:11,31
[19] Acts 10:34; Romans 2:11

Him. He justifies the ungodly. But Rahab's story didn't end there. The conquest of Jericho marked only the beginning, for she had now found God. Her life began to blossom. There was no further longing for her former occupation; instead, she became an honorable housewife. She, a heathen woman, lived among the Jewish people, married the Israelite Salmon, and had a child.[20] If we were to evaluate her effectiveness as a mother by her sympathetic and wise son, Boaz, the husband of Ruth, then she did very well indeed, for Ruth became the great-grandmother of King David.[21] Because of her faith, Rahab became a mother in the lineage of Jesus Christ, the Messiah.

---

[20] Joshua 6:25; Matthew 1:5
[21] The Book of Ruth and Matthew 1:5-16

4

THE JEWISH MAID

The Girl Who Talked About God

The question for each man to settle is not what he would do
for the Lord if he had more money, time, or education, but
what he will do with the things he has. It's not who you are or
what you have that matters—but whether Christ controls you.

AUTHOR UNKNOWN

READ

2 Kings 5:1-5,14-17; Acts 1:8

• • •

850 BC. OFFICIALLY THERE WAS PEACE IN ISRAEL. However,
the troops of Syria's King Ben-hadad kept making raids into
Israel to capture prisoners as spoil. One day they captured a
young Jewish girl who was likely not more than fifteen years
old.[1] Her name is not recorded in the Bible. Perhaps this is
because what is told about her is so impressive that her name
is of secondary importance.

The girl became the maid of the wife of a high-ranking
officer in the king's army. The officer, Naaman, was capable

---

[1] 2 Kings 5:2

and very influential. He was greatly honored by the king because of his valor in combat.[2] Was it a result of the prayers of her God-fearing parents, or was it the answer to her own heart's cry to God that the little maid arrived, probably via the slave market in Damascus, in this good home?

At the moment, Naaman was deeply worried. A shadow had fallen over his house that couldn't be driven away. He had leprosy, the most dreadful of diseases. Once a person contracted leprosy, he was an outcast for the rest of his life.[3] It was a horrible disease, and it might take years before death freed the sufferer from his isolation.

Naaman was a dead man already. His physical death might be many years in the future, but in reality—for his wife, his master, his colleagues, and the little maid—he would soon no longer exist. No king, no trophy of victory could prevent his expulsion. He would be forced to wander outside the city walls as a beggar. Everyone who came near him would be warned to stay away.

Naaman and his wife had tried to keep the illness a secret, but now this was no longer possible. The secret had become known—even the maid was aware of the shocking situation.

She had not become bitter because of her captivity. Her faith in God, learned in her parents' home, had kept her from that. She submitted to her superiors and found herself sympathetic to them. They, recognizing this, confided in her.

[2] 2 Kings 5:1
[3] Leviticus 13:45-46 is an illustration of this principle in Israel; historically, lepers were outcasts in all societies.

Have you ever dealt with bitterness because of a situation or person in your life? What was your relationship with God like during that time? How do you think increased faith could have changed your perspective?

Yes, they had a problem. But, she thought, didn't problems exist so that they could be taken to God? Didn't these Syrians know that God had a servant on earth—Elisha? He was a greatly honored figure in her parental home. So she came to her mistress with a very natural proposal: "Why doesn't my lord go visit the prophet who is in Samaria? He can cure him of his leprosy."[4]

Do you automatically turn to God in troubled times? If so, then what results do you observe in your life and in your relationships? If no, why not?

Just a few words, but what a difference they made. Instead of certain death, there was a possibility of life! Her mistress took her words seriously, and her master thought they were important enough to pass on to the king. The king ordered immediate action. As soon as possible, Naaman was on his way, bearing many gifts, to see the prophet Elisha in Samaria.[5]

[4] 2 Kings 5:3, author's paraphrase
[5] 2 Kings 5:4-6

When Naaman returned, not only was he healed of the dreaded disease—his skin clean and without spot, looking like the healthy skin of a young boy—but the healing process had also gone far deeper. His heart had been touched. He now had confidence in the God of Israel. He said, "I know that there is no God in all the earth but in Israel." Instead of worshiping idols, he became a worshiper of the living God.[6]

Nothing more is said about the young girl whose life was described in two sentences. Yet some aspects of her life are striking.

The young maid may never have seen her own situation redeemed. She may have remained a slave, far from home for the rest of her life. How do you respond when God's hand of rescue seems to touch everyone but you?

First, she must have been an excellent servant who did her work well. Someone once said, "Your actions speak so loudly that I cannot hear what you are saying." She lived too early in history to have read James' words that a person's faith is proven by his deeds,[7] yet she practiced what James preached. Her deeds had prepared an opening for her words. Her master and mistress took her seriously.

[6] 2 Kings 5:14-17
[7] James 2:14,26

Do your deeds open pathways for your words about who God is? If not, why do you think that is? If works don't provide salvation but do illustrate faith, what sort of heart work do you need to do with the Lord to exhibit the deeds of His power in your life?

Second, she did not keep silent out of shyness. She didn't think she was too young to have something significant to say.[8] She didn't feel that her position was too low for her to be heard. Instead, she saw a person in need and believed that the God of Israel could meet the need. She trusted that He would heal Naaman of his terrible disease. That was all she said, a few simple words, but the result was significant. A whole new future opened up to Naaman.

What things keep you from speaking up when you sense God wanting to use you in a situation? Your age, social status, personality, gender?

A few simple words brought new life to a man, hope for his family, and support for his king. A few simple words gave attention and brought honor to the God of Israel. This little maid continues to speak to people today through the words

---
[8] 1 Timothy 4:12

that were recorded through the guidance of the Holy Spirit long after she died. History can never blot out what she said and did.

———————

Compare what the girl did with the commission Jesus gave in Acts 1:8. What lessons do you draw from her boldness? How can you show boldness in your own life?

———————

She didn't say much, but what she said revealed her faith—a faith that was tested by reality and served the people around her. Because of her faith a life was changed. The insignificant little maid was not so insignificant!

5

RUTH

A Woman Characterized by Loyalty

Every woman has the special privilege to be a "power-station" for God to be used in any human dilemma. More than anything, people need loving. They thirst for LOVE.

BROTHER MANDUS, *FOR WOMEN ONLY: WITH MANKIND IN MIND*

READ

Ruth 2:1-23; Ruth 3:1; Ruth 4:13; for the full story, read the entire book of Ruth

• • •

RUTH WORKED WITHOUT STOPPING, hardly allowing herself a break. Sweat trickled down her back as the sun became increasingly hot. Steadily, the little heap of grain she was gleaning grew. She paused and sat down in the shade for a rest, but not for long. She wanted to surprise her mother-in-law, Naomi, with a good supply of grain.

Suddenly footsteps approached, and a male voice addressed her kindly. Looking up, she saw the face of a man who was no longer young. She recognized him right away. Boaz, the owner of the land.[1]

"Listen, my daughter," he said. "Stay right here with us to glean; don't think of going to any other fields. Stay right behind my women workers. I have warned the young men not to bother you. When you are thirsty, go and help yourself to the water."[2]

His friendliness and care and the warmth of his words took her by surprise. She fell to her knees, bowing. "W-why are you paying attention to me?" she stammered. "You are so kind. Don't you know that I am a foreigner?"[3] *He doesn't treat me like a beggar*, she thought. *Instead, he talks to me like he would to one of his women workers who earns her own living.*

"Yes, I know," Boaz replied. "I am well aware of all that you did for your mother-in-law after the death of your husband. I also know that you left your father and your mother and your home country to live as a foreigner among our people."[4]

What a kind man, Ruth thought. She began to trust his friendliness, which she had noticed after his arrival from Bethlehem. He was rich, but he treated his workers fairly and cordially. "May the Lord be with you!" he often said to them, to which they answered, "The LORD bless you!"[5] *Is this a phrase reflecting pious politeness, a way of greeting one another in this religious country?* she had wondered. *Or is it the result of Boaz's close touch with God?*

Then Boaz spoke to her again. "The LORD repay you for

---

[1] Ruth 2:3
[2] Ruth 2:8-9, author's paraphrase
[3] Ruth 2:10, author's paraphrase
[4] Ruth 2:11, author's paraphrase
[5] Ruth 2:4, author's paraphrase

what you have done, and a full reward be given you by the LORD, the God of Israel, under whose wings you have come to take refuge!"[6]

It struck Ruth how naturally he talked about God. *He does it in the same way as Naomi*, she mused. That type of relationship with God had always impressed her. *This man has indeed taken God into his considerations. I can taste that in his words and the seriousness with which he speaks. He, of all people, understands why I have come to this country. He is right. I want to find shelter under the wings of the God of Israel.*

What do you think it means for people to taste God in your words? Do you exhibit that sort of attitude and way of speaking to others?

"Your words are quite after my heart, sir," she said simply. "You are indeed very kind to me, and I am not even one of your workers."[7]

After several more hours of hard work, it was time to eat. Modestly, Ruth stayed away from the reapers. She knew her place.

Once again Boaz called her to the fore. "Come here," he called. "Eat with us."[8] After she came over, he watched personally to make sure that she received enough to eat. He cared for her till she had eaten enough.

---

[6] Ruth 2:12, ESV
[7] Ruth 2:13, author's paraphrase
[8] Ruth 2:14, author's paraphrase

She managed to disguise the combined fear and excitement she felt, for she knew that Hebrew men normally had little to do with women in public, much less with a foreign woman. *Yet he is treating me like a woman of high birth, like his equal,* she thought with surprise, *even though I am a newcomer in his land.*

Those around her quickly appreciated Ruth. From the moment she set foot on Boaz's soil, she had made an impression through her loyalty, courtesy, modest manners, and desire to work. Although she was a foreigner, she could easily have made demands because of her position as daughter-in-law of the prominent Naomi. She could have pressured people for her rights under Hebrew law, which required the Israelites to help poor and foreign people.[9]

In what ways is your reputation a direct reflection of your actions?

Ruth, however, didn't demand anything. She asked humbly for permission to glean ears of grain and showed deep gratitude to everyone for every favor that was extended to her. She was, furthermore, diligent in her responsibilities.

Boaz was not the only person to notice her right away; she also made a good impression on the foreman of the work crew. So in a country where it was routine for women to draw water for men, she drank from the water that the servants had drawn.[10]

---

[9] Leviticus 19:9-10
[10] Ruth 2:9

Word of her loyalty would soon spread. People in Bethlehem, for example, would talk about the Moabite woman who cared so well for her mother-in-law. She would be known as the foreigner who had dignity, a spirit of inspiration, and concern and love toward others.

Ruth finally stopped working when evening came. After she beat out the barley she had gleaned, she had nearly an entire bushel.[11]

Did she notice that her work in the afternoon had gone more smoothly than it had in the morning? Did she realize that the servants, under orders from Boaz, had snapped off some heads of barley and deliberately dropped them?[12]

Picking up the heavy load of grain, she made her way from Boaz's field to the city. Tired, satisfied, and grateful, she arrived at Naomi's.[13]

"So much?" Naomi said happily when she saw how much grain Ruth was carrying. "Where have you been? For whom did you work? May God bless the man who has been so kind to you!"[14] Her questions tumbled out without stopping.

Ruth's story came out in bits and pieces. Naomi became excited about what her daughter-in-law had said. She learned what had taken place that day. She heard all about what Boaz had said and done and how Ruth had been personally invited to keep coming back to glean till the entire field had been harvested.[15]

---

[11] Ruth 2:17
[12] Ruth 2:16
[13] Ruth 2:18
[14] Ruth 2:19, author's paraphrase
[15] Ruth 2:21

"That man is our close relative,"[16] Naomi exclaimed after she had heard the whole story. Surprise rang in her voice, and hope. She was impressed that God had led Ruth so clearly from the very first day. Boaz was a link with the past. Would he also become a bridge to a new future?

Throughout the following weeks, Ruth went to the field every morning till the barley and wheat harvests were over.[17] Although she had gleaned enough food on that first day to last her for weeks, she did not slow down. She never made claims to the fact that she was related to rich Boaz. Fulfilling her tasks without pretensions, she was faithful to the given promise that she wouldn't leave Naomi alone.

What does faithfulness look like in the daily tasks you have before you? To the people in your life?

Seven or eight weeks had passed by swiftly, and as usual, all the workers celebrated the end of the harvest season with an elaborate meal. After eating and drinking his fill, Boaz lay down to sleep on the threshing floor in order to keep watch over his grain.

This was the ideal situation that Naomi had been waiting for.[18] According to Hebrew law, a widow without children had the right of a levirate marriage. In order to keep the name of a deceased husband intact, Moses had instituted

---

[16] Ruth 2:20
[17] Ruth 2:23
[18] Ruth 3:2

that the brother who was next to the dead husband in age should then marry the widow. The first son born out of that marriage would then continue the original family line of the deceased so that his name would not be forgotten.[19] As far as Naomi knew, Boaz was the closest relative with whom Ruth could claim her rights, for Elimelek had no living brothers. Naomi was not only mindful of the continuation of the name and descendants of her husband and sons, but she was also interested in Ruth's happiness. She had carefully watched the course of events of the past weeks and could not help but clearly see God's leading in them.

She and Ruth had arrived in Bethlehem at the beginning of the harvest. Without even knowing it, they had gone straight to the land of Boaz. And of course, even as an outsider Naomi had immediately detected the first signs of kindled love. These seemed to be signs that God was using the circumstances to bring Ruth and Boaz together.

Often we don't see God's fingerprints on the circumstances of life until much later. Reflect on a time in the past when you now see that God was active in your circumstances. How does that make you feel about your relationship with Him?

Naomi also recognized similarities between the relationship Ruth and Boaz had and the marriages of her prominent

---

[19] Deuteronomy 25:5-10

ancestors. Since his mother was also a non-Israelite woman,[20] Boaz seemed to be a suitable husband for Ruth. She in turn would be a good helper for him. This was the norm God had established for Eve, the first woman.[21]

Aspects of their relationship also turned Naomi's thoughts back to the patriarch Abraham and his wife, Sarah. And like Rebekah, the wife of Isaac, and Rachel, one of Jacob's wives, Ruth had come into contact with a godly man through her desire to work diligently. Undoubtedly, the love of the man for the woman, which had formed the seal of those earlier covenants,[22] was also present in Boaz.

The next thing Naomi had to do was check whether God was opening or closing doors. So she came up with a proposal based on three factors: fulfillment of God's laws, her love for Ruth, and her perception of the Holy Spirit's leading.

How do you discern God's will in a situation? What in Naomi's approach could be applicable to your own life?

"Take a bath, use some perfume, and put on a nice dress. Then go to the threshing floor tonight," Naomi said. "Be sure that Boaz doesn't notice you before he has finished his supper. Watch where he lies down to sleep and then quietly

[20] Joshua 6:25; Matthew 1:5
[21] Genesis 2:18
[22] Genesis 24:67; 29:20

lie down at his feet. After that he will make it clear what you have to do further."[23]

Ruth, schooled in the Moabite culture, thought that this was a strange suggestion. She was willing to follow Israelite law, but she was a modest woman; she was also high spirited and dared to make far-reaching decisions. Above all, she loved chastity and purity.

But she also had a deep respect for Naomi and believed that Naomi would do anything she could to make her happy. She knew that Naomi would not make a wrong proposal and would not suggest anything dishonorable. She knew that Naomi reckoned with God, and it would be wise to listen to her advice.

Have you cultivated relationships with women who exhibit depth of relationship with God? If so, what roles have those women played in your life? If not, who is a woman of godly wisdom and discernment with whom you might develop a friendship?

"Your people will be my people and your God my God,"[24] Ruth had declared to Naomi on the road to Bethlehem. Now it was time to adapt herself to the laws of this land and the God in whom she had taken refuge. He would watch over her. He would not forsake her, even now. Trusting Him, she decided to do what Naomi had proposed.

[23] Ruth 3:3-4, author's paraphrase
[24] Ruth 1:16

Ruth also had a deep respect for Boaz. He was the man who, without her even asking, had proven to be her protector and provider. Hadn't he already shown that he understood her? He was a man who walked closely with God. He wouldn't hurt her or cause her pain.

"I will do whatever you say,"[25] she answered Naomi. That night she lay down at Boaz's feet. She waited expectantly, wondering how Boaz would react.

Around midnight Boaz woke up and was startled to find a woman lying at his feet. Ruth then told him her story, simply and clearly. "On the basis of God's law, I ask that I may be your wife, for you are my closest relative."[26]

Boaz's reaction touched her deeply. He showed again how much he understood her. She was moved by his humility.

Overlooking the fact that he himself was a desirable suitor, Boaz talked about Ruth's faithfulness to her deceased husband. He touched on her purity in dealing with men and praised her virtues that were known to everyone in the city.[27]

What men in your life show the sort of character and respectful treatment of women that Boaz exhibited? If you are married, how can you honor your husband for such character? If you are single, how can you honor the men in your life (fathers, brothers, friends) for such character?

---

[25] Ruth 3:5
[26] Ruth 3:9, author's paraphrase
[27] Ruth 3:10-11

He continued by saying that he was willing to marry her. There was a problem, however, for another man was more closely related to Ruth than he was. If that man waived his rights by not redeeming her, then the way was free for him. Through this test, God would clearly show which of the two men He intended to be Ruth's husband.

Ruth didn't need to go through the trying experience of offering herself once again to a man. Boaz would arrange that for her. Once more he showed his concern for her. He would not send her away in the middle of the night.[28]

Early in the morning while it was still dark, Ruth left Boaz and went out into the empty streets. Boaz had not touched her. His deep love and respect for her had been expressed through his control over his desires.

He had also protected her good name. No one would need to know that she had been on the threshing floor. If this fact should ever become known, it would damage her reputation and she would not be a suitable partner for a redeemer.[29]

Study Ruth's relationship with Boaz thoughtfully. Do you think God led them to each other? If so, why? Do you see the foundation of a happy marriage in this story? Describe your reason(s). How are the characteristics of their relationship applicable to your life?

---

[28] Ruth 3:12-13
[29] Ruth 3:14

Not only did Boaz guard himself against evil, but he was also conscious of the ideas that other people might have. His conversation and attitude proved that God was foremost in his thoughts.

Ruth walked quietly through the city, thinking. *It is just like the first time I met him. Then it was during an orderly working day, but now it has been an unexpected situation at night.* Now she was sure that Boaz was close to God and knew in her heart that she could entrust herself to such a man.

How does trust in God pave the way for trust in others? Does your relationship with God help you discern the level of trust you may place in those around you?

As she was leaving, Boaz had handed her a bushel and a half of barley.[30] "You should not arrive at your mother-in-law's empty-handed," he had said. By this act, Boaz communicated two promises to Ruth. When he married her, he would not forget Naomi. He also pledged, in view of their future marriage, a small portion of her bridal gift. If for some reason Ruth would meet someone on her way home, this token of his care for her would serve as a reasonable explanation for her early-morning walk.

Boaz, whose name may have meant "fleetness," lived up

[30] Ruth 3:15

to his name. That very day he settled all necessary details according to the rules of the law.[31] Energetically, he met with the other relative—the potential redeemer of Ruth—at the gate of the city. Then he called together ten elders of the city and held a meeting. After the other man decided not to marry Ruth because such a marriage might jeopardize his inheritance, Boaz bought Naomi's land before witnesses. This made him responsible for the inheritance of her husband and her sons. He became Ruth's legal husband and promised that a future son would carry the family name of her first husband.

The bride was a woman of exceptional qualities. She was brave, having dared to exchange a well-known present for an unknown future. She was stalwart and had developed initiative, but at the same time was willing to listen to others' advice. She was loyal and kept her promises. Industrious, humble, and pure, she was known throughout the city for her radiating love. The bridegroom had undivided attention for her. He respected her. Because of his love, he protected and cared for her.

What characteristics do you observe in Ruth that you wish to see strengthened in your own life? Submit those desires to the Lord, asking Him to cultivate those things in you.

---

[31] Ruth 4:1-10

A remarkable relationship based on understanding existed between the two partners. They could talk with each other and knew how to listen. Lack of communication—the dangerous rock on which many marriages are broken up—did not threaten them. Their mutual respect and desire to further the other's interests guaranteed a happy marriage. This marriage had the characteristics of a covenant made in heaven.

Ruth, the woman who loved God and her fellow man, experienced God's favor. Her son, Obed, was chosen by Him to become a forefather in the lineage of Jesus, the Messiah.[32] The privilege every Hebrew woman was hoping for was extended to her. She became a mother in the line of the Redeemer.

Christians the world over should gratefully recognize Ruth's contribution. The Messiah, the redeemer of Israel, is also the Savior of the world. Through Ruth, Hebrew and Christian are forever united. Ruth's influence, far from being restricted to the Hebrew land and people, permeates human history up to the present day.

---

[32] Matthew 1:5-16

6
MARY

The Most Privileged Among Women

My heart is overflowing with praise of my Lord, my soul is full of joy in God my Saviour. For he has deigned to notice me, his humble servant and, after this, all the people who ever shall be will call me the happiest of women!

MARY, LUKE 1:46-48, PH

READ

Luke 1:26-38; Matthew 1:18-25; Luke 2:6-14,17-19,33-35; John 19:25-27

• • •

"I-I AM THE LORD'S SERVANT, and I will do whatever He desires,"[1] Mary stammered, totally overwhelmed by the message the angel had just brought. In her thoughts, she reviewed what he had said. She, Mary, would become the mother of the Messiah! The Redeemer who had been promised first to Adam, then more clearly to Abraham, and who was later foretold by various prophets, would be brought into the world by her.

---

[1] Luke 1:38, author's paraphrase

53

She realized that He would be coming. Every Jewish woman had hoped it would be her privilege to be the mother of the Messiah. And now His time had come—and she had been chosen to be His mother. She had never dreamed she would be the one.

Study Mary's Magnificat (Luke 1:46-55).
What were her thoughts about God?
How did she think about herself?

She was young, and she came from a very insignificant village.[2] And—how could she give birth to a baby? Why, she wasn't even married! She was only engaged. It is no wonder she replied, "But I am a virgin and not even married. How can this happen?"[3]

The angel had begun with, "Don't be afraid, Mary, for God has chosen to bless you." Then he had told her how the Holy Spirit would work this miracle in her. Her child would be called the Son of God.[4]

Mary knew God through the books of Moses, the Psalms, and the writings of the prophets. She had a deep reverence for the Lord God in her heart because she knew what He had done in the history of her people. She was aware of what He had done not only for the entire nation but for certain people as well.

[2] John 1:46-47
[3] Luke 1:35, author's paraphrase
[4] Luke 1:30-32

*How does reflecting on God's work not only
in your past but also throughout history
impact your faith? What specific things has
He done that have strengthened your faith?*

She knew of His graciousness toward those who revered Him and that He preferred to work through those who had no worldly might. She was well aware of the fact that she had no position or wealth. Was that the reason that He had selected her? Was she a usable instrument because she could claim no worldly honor in and of herself?

*Are you a usable instrument for the Lord?
In what ways might worldly honor be keeping
you from being willing to be used by Him?*

Mary was willing to sacrifice herself to become His lowliest servant. "May everything you said come true,"[5] she said simply, gazing at the departing angel.

These words indicated complete surrender on her part. She was not holding anything back.

It was not an ill-considered answer. Her Son, the One who had just been announced, would utter practically the same words in Gethsemane: "Not as I will, but as you will."[6] In the future she would have ample opportunity to prove that

---

[5] Luke 1:38, author's paraphrase
[6] Matthew 26:39

she meant just what she said. However, at that moment she could not foresee the consequences.

Mary, the most privileged among women, learned from the very beginning that exceptional privilege often goes hand in hand with sacrifice. Moses had experienced this before her.[7] Paul would after her.[8]

Reflect on the difference between the privilege of the world and the privilege of God. What examples can you think of in which sacrifice was intimately tied to the privilege of God?

The first thing she sacrificed was her reputation. She exchanged this in order to be available to God. This created a problem for Joseph, her fiancé. He was a man who walked with God. How could he possibly marry a girl who was expecting a baby by someone else?

Because he loved her, he didn't want to accuse her openly, for if he did, Mary would be put to death.[9] The Law stated that if a Hebrew bride had betrayed her husband and was not a virgin at marriage, she was to be stoned without pardon.[10]

Therefore, Joseph planned to leave her quietly. Did he want to give the problem of what should happen to her back to God? If so, he would be putting the problem back where it belonged.

---

[7] Hebrews 11:24-26
[8] Acts 9:10-16
[9] Matthew 1:19
[10] Deuteronomy 22:20-21

Too often we place ourselves in the position of judge and jury. What are specific situations right now in which you need to give people back to God, where they belong?

In a dream the angel of the Lord disclosed the true nature of the situation to Joseph. Mary was pregnant with the promised Immanuel about whom Isaiah had prophesied.[11]

Joseph would also be a privileged person as the child's earthly father. He would be the one to give the child His name, Jesus. It was to be his honor to educate the child as if He were his own son. Joseph's house was to be the house where the Son of God, during His time on earth, would feel most comfortable. For Jesus, it was to be His only earthly home.

Joseph married Mary. He had to sacrifice some personal happiness in exchange for the honor bestowed on him. Not only was he marrying a woman whose purity was questioned by those around them, but he was also to have no sexual relations with her until after Jesus was born.[12]

. . .

Together Joseph and Mary climbed the steps of the temple Square in Jerusalem. They carried the child and a pair of turtledoves to offer to the Lord.[13]

[11] Isaiah 7:14; Matthew 1:20-21
[12] Matthew 1:24-25
[13] Luke 2:22-24

Mary thought over the past year's events. She remembered how, soon after the visit of the angel Gabriel, she had gone to a small village near Jerusalem to visit her relative Elizabeth, who had also been expecting a baby.

Without Mary mentioning a word about her own pregnancy, Elizabeth had welcomed her as blessed among women. Filled with the Holy Spirit, Elizabeth had called her "the mother of my Lord."[14]

Mary recalled her own reaction. It had been a burst of praise to God, a song of praise that He had put in her heart.[15] She had been deeply impressed by the magnitude of the things that were going to happen. People would call her blessed throughout future generations. Not because of herself, but because of what God had done. He was great, holy, and almighty. She was unworthy of this. She had nothing to offer but her gratitude and praise. The child to be born would also be her Savior. (Though she felt privileged, she also realized that she too was a sinner who needed the Savior.)

When the delivery of the child was at hand, Mary and Joseph made the long journey from Nazareth to Bethlehem, the ancient home of King David, forefather of them both, to be registered for a census that Caesar Augustus had ordered to be taken throughout the nation.[16] As they had expected, every inn was full. Bethlehem, situated on the caravan route from Jerusalem to Hebron, was a very busy city.

Her child was born outside the city in a cave where farm

[14] Luke 1:39-45
[15] Luke 1:46-55
[16] Luke 2:1-5

animals were kept in the winter. She was sad that her Son didn't even have a bed to sleep on His first night on earth.[17]

While she and Joseph had been alone and lonely, another miracle was occurring elsewhere. A bright light shone in the night—a light brighter than day. Suddenly a great army of angels appeared to shepherds in the fields nearby. "Glory to God in the highest heaven, and on earth peace" they sung as they proclaimed the birth of God's Son, the Savior of the world.[18]

Times when we are alone and lonely are often when we see God's work most clearly. Like Mary and Joseph, have you ever seen the obvious work of God in a time when you were alone and lonely? What did that do to your perspective about that time?

The shepherds, appointed by the angels, came to the stable.[19] They were poor men with weather-beaten faces. Later, rich and learned men came from the East. They had made a long journey to bring honor and precious gifts of gold, frankincense, and costly oil.[20] In this way her Son had been announced by God and welcomed by rich and poor alike.

Mary sat quietly, not knowing quite what to say, her heart absorbed in all these precious memories.

Suddenly, as they brought their Son into the temple, a very

[17] Luke 2:6-7
[18] Luke 2:8-14
[19] Luke 2:15-16
[20] Matthew 2:1-12

old man approached them and took the child from them.[21]
The old man was Simeon, a devout man who had been waiting for the coming of the Messiah for a long time. "You have
kept Your promise, Lord. Now You may let Your servant go
in peace," they heard him say, much to their amazement. He
continued. "For I have seen Him as You promised I would.
I have seen the Savior You have given to the world."[22]

The Holy Spirit had guided the old man's speech. There
was no longer any question in the minds of Joseph and Mary
that they were holding the Son of God in their arms.

Anna, an elderly prophetess, who had, like Simeon, spent
most of her adult life in the presence of God, also recognized
the child as the promised Messiah and left for the city to tell
the people that the redemption of Jerusalem was at hand.[23]

Simeon had also said something else remarkable to Mary:
"Listen carefully. This child shall be rejected by many in
Israel, but He will be of the greatest joy to many others.
The deepest thoughts of many hearts shall be revealed, but a
sword shall pierce your soul."[24]

It wasn't long before the first sorrow came. King Herod had
all boys two years and younger in Bethlehem murdered, hoping to kill the announced King of the Jews.[25] Joseph and his
little family escaped because God had warned them. They were
forced, however, to take a long trip through the inhospitable
Negev Desert, a country virtually without food and water.
What made this journey to Egypt even more difficult for Mary

[21] Luke 2:25-28
[22] Luke 2:29-32, author's paraphrase
[23] Luke 2:36-38
[24] Luke 2:34-35, author's paraphrase
[25] Matthew 2:13-16

was the knowledge that many children were being murdered because of her Son. In her mind she heard the cries of the innocent babies who were being brutally slaughtered. Being a new mother herself, she easily identified with the pain of the mothers of those children. The mother of the Son of God was finding that great joy was mingled with many tears.

• • •

Ten years had passed.

It was very crowded and busy in Jerusalem. Entire families were there to celebrate the feast of the Passover in the Holy City and to honor the Lord God with sacrifices.[26]

It was a happy occasion, for they were able to worship the Lord in the company of old friends they only met on such festive days. Because of the large number of families visiting the city, it was teeming with children.

The adults enjoyed their too-rare contact with relatives and friends from far away. They walked and talked loudly with one another in the streets. The children twittered like young birds as they danced and frolicked together. It was easy for the absence of a child to go unnoticed in such a multitude. The parents would naturally assume that the child was in the company of others somewhere else in the group.

That was why Joseph and Mary did not discover until after a full, tiring day on the homeward journey that Jesus was not with them. He was nowhere to be found. Finally, heavy hearted, they returned to Jerusalem to search for Him.

---
[26] Luke 2:41-51

They looked everywhere, without success.

Finally, after three days of searching, they found Him in the temple. To their amazement, the young Jesus was seated among the highly learned rabbis. He was not just listening to them; he was asking them questions as well. He surprised them with His intelligence, understanding, and properly spoken answers.

Mary was upset. "Son," she rebuked Him, "why have You done this? Your father and I have been searching for You all over Jerusalem." His answer was not unfriendly, but clear and without reserve: "You shouldn't have had to search. Didn't you know I would be in My Father's house?"[27]

His father? But Joseph had been looking for Him everywhere, along with His mother. Hadn't she understood that He was talking about His heavenly Father?

Jesus was beginning to grow away from them. He was beginning His life's journey toward His true destiny. While He was their lost son today, He was also the Son of God, the Redeemer of a lost world. The ties between Him and His family had already begun to loosen.

Did this experience remind Mary of Simeon's words? Was she experiencing the initial pains of the sword that would finally pierce her heart?

When they returned to Nazareth, everything appeared to be unchanged. Jesus was obedient to them as before. But something had happened in Mary's heart. She kept this memory and recorded it with the others in her heart. She was being given the opportunity to subject her motherly desires to the will of God.

[27] Luke 2:48-49, author's paraphrase

What desire is God asking you to subject to His will? What would doing so look like?

Their years together were good as Jesus grew from youth to manhood. His mother's influence upon Him during that time was great.

"Jesus grew in wisdom and stature, and in favor with God and man."[28] Jesus, the Son of God, who was perfect as a child, developed naturally into a man. This is a holy mystery, how God as a man on earth could submit Himself to the influence of Mary.

Jesus did not grow up in a rich or socially privileged family. But His spiritual environment was enviable. Both His parents walked with God and respected each other. Mary's thoughts, especially, were full of God.

A person's thoughts determine his or her deeds. Following that principle, Joseph and Mary strove to make their home and the education of their children conform to the thoughts of God. There was a friendly atmosphere in that tiny home in Nazareth. It was permeated with a spirit of true humility and a natural devoutness. It was a spirit that made it easy for the children to obey their parents. It was in the home of Joseph and Mary that Jesus first encountered the Scriptures. His mother's love for the Word of God was an example to her Son.

---

[28] Luke 2:52

Does the atmosphere of your life, and particularly your thought life, determine your deeds? How can you make the atmosphere of your home and relationships conform more to the thoughts of God?

For eighteen more years, Jesus lived in His parents' home. More children were born. There were other sons—James, Joseph, Simon, and Judas—and daughters also.[29] Since Joseph died during this period, it is very likely that Jesus, as the eldest son, shared His mother's family problems and was responsible for the family's livelihood.

People no longer called Him the carpenter's son. He was now the carpenter.[30]

When Jesus was thirty years old, everything changed. Mary saw this clearly when she attended a wedding feast with Him in Cana, a little village near Nazareth nestled in the rolling hills of the Galilean countryside.[31] She noticed that the host was embarrassed because the wine had run out. Her first reaction was to relay the problem to her firstborn. Then she made a painful discovery. Her Son seemed to be changed. He was not behaving like the obedient Son she knew so well.

"Woman," He replied, "what do I have to do with you?"[32] Addressing her as "woman" did not indicate a lack of respect or

---

[29] Matthew 13:55-56
[30] Mark 6:3
[31] John 2:1-11
[32] John 2:4, author's paraphrase

unfriendliness. Hebrew women were used to being addressed that way. But it clearly marked a distance between Him and His mother. *When has He ever treated me in such a manner before?* she wondered. Then her memories went back to that day in the temple. At that time He had indicated in much the same way that He, though her Son, was not able to obey every one of her orders. He had higher orders to follow.

Mary was not touchy, and if she was uncomfortable she didn't show it. "Do whatever He tells you,"[33] she said to the servants, for she knew that He was God and could work miracles.

She seemed to be willing to take second place. Did she already understand that He would later be teaching about the high priority God put on serving?[34]

Our willingness to take second place is an outcome of our faith. As you have grown in your relationship with God, have you observed your heart change in this way? If so, how? If not, what seems to hold you back from taking second place?

When His ministry began, He left Mary for good. From then on He was not primarily the Son of Mary, but Jesus of Nazareth, about whom the entire country had begun to talk, for the Son of God went around the countryside doing good.

[33] John 2:5
[34] Matthew 23:11-12

Mary learned to draw back, yet not without pain. Increasingly she experienced the cutting edge of the sword in her life, but she also realized that her sorrow was bound up with the favor of God. All that remained for her to do was to make herself available to Him again and again.

As Jesus moved throughout the countryside, healing the sick and preaching the gospel, Mary's faith in Him found opportunity to grow. It was no doubt painful to her that her other sons didn't believe in Him,[35] and that the people of Nazareth would not accept Him.[36] He made this painfully clear to her when she and her sons tried to talk with Him. When He was told, "Your mother and brothers are standing outside, wanting to speak to you," He answered, "Who is my mother, and who are my brothers?" Then, while pointing to His disciples, He added, "Whoever does the will of my Father in heaven is my brother and sister and mother."[37]

The men with whom He mixed daily and His followers were equal to her. Relationships were no longer tested by the bond of blood, but by the bond of shared faith in God.

What is the defining aspect of your relationships? Blood? Faith? Shared interests? Evaluate honestly. If the bond of shared faith does not define your deepest relationships, why do you think that is?

---

[35] John 7:3-5
[36] Luke 4:16-30
[37] Matthew 12:46-50

The sword pierced through her soul with all of its sharpness when she stood at the foot of the cross on which her Son hung like a common criminal.[38]

Here Mary reached the height of her suffering.

She didn't try to ignore it or try to make it easy for herself. Like Him, she also drank the bitter cup of suffering to the final drop. She was with Him till His final moment. She saw His agony and heard Him scoffed at and mocked.

The hours passed slowly in the scorching sun, and Someone—the most beloved of all—suffered as no other man could ever suffer.

Mary stood beneath the cross and suffered with Him. This was part of motherhood. The words she had spoken to the angel Gabriel still echoed in her mind: "May everything you said come true."[39] She held on only because she had made herself totally available to the Lord. How she felt was secondary.

It can be difficult—and frightening—to make ourselves totally available to the Lord. What might be holding you back from making your feelings and desires secondary to His?

Jesus saw her, and though in agony of death, He did not forget to take care of her. "Woman, here is your son," she

[38] John 19:25
[39] Luke 1:38, author's paraphrase

heard Him say. And then He said to John, the disciple whom Jesus loved[40], "Here is your mother."[41]

Jesus hadn't left His earthly life without taking good care of His mother. The man and the woman who on earth were the nearest to Him would best be able to understand and help each other after He was gone. From then on, Mary lived in John's home.

The cross is not Mary's last appearance in Scripture. She appears again with Jesus' disciples, several other women, and her other sons after Christ's ascension. In the upper room in Jerusalem, Mary dedicated herself, like the others, to consistent prayer.[42]

Though she had lost her Son, she did not concern herself with her personal loss but accepted that her task regarding Him had been fulfilled.

Mary, the woman most blessed and most privileged of all women, whose name was more greatly honored than that of any other mortal, dedicated herself anew to God. Again she had no claim. Inconspicuously, she took her place among the others. Mary knew that she could overlook personal interests and dedicated herself wholly to the honor of God.

Mary had become a mature woman. In the last thirty years of her life, she had reached unknown pinnacles of happiness. At the same time, she had experienced deep heart sorrows that no other woman ever has or ever will encounter. But her attitude toward God hadn't changed. She had proven

[40] John 13:23
[41] John 19:26-27
[42] Acts 1:9-14

with her life that she meant the words she spoke when the Messiah was announced: "I am the Lord's servant, and I will do whatever He desires."[43]

We see in Mary an utter commitment to believing in God's goodness and trusting His will no matter the circumstances. Too often, we let our circumstances define how we feel about God. Which Scripture can you rest in to help you cling fast to His character and promises regardless of your circumstances?

---

[43] Luke 1:38, author's paraphrase

7

ELIZABETH

A Woman of Strong Character

A capable, intelligent, and virtuous woman—who is he who can find her? She is far more precious than jewels and her value is far above rubies or pearls.

SOLOMON, PROVERBS 31:10, AMP

READ

Luke 1:5-20,24-25,39-45

• • •

ELIZABETH WAS A REMARKABLE WOMAN. She was the wife of a priest. Priests were only allowed to marry pious women whose moral behavior was totally blameless.[1] Otherwise, the wives would defile their husbands' holy ministries. Elizabeth was a woman beyond reproach.

Not only was she married to a priest, but she herself was a descendant of the distinguished tribe of Aaron.[2] Her name was derived from the same root word as that of Aaron's wife, Elisheba.[3]

---

[1] Leviticus 21:1-7
[2] Luke 1:5
[3] Exodus 6:23

The Bible stresses that they were both righteous before God, walking blamelessly in all the commandments and ordinances of the Lord.[4]

No one spoke badly of her. She didn't simply follow in the spiritual wake of her pious husband; she had an independently developed spiritual life and was honored because of her personal relationship with God.

Oftentimes it can become easy to rest on friends or family to help us coast spiritually. Do you have an independently developed spiritual life, or do you rely on others to pull you through spiritual things?

Not only did Elizabeth live to the letter of the Law, but she also served God in the spirit of the Law. In light of all this, her childlessness was enigmatic and painful to her. Like Eve and every Jewish mother who had brought children into the world since, Elizabeth had hoped to become the mother of the Messiah. Yet the blessing of children had been withheld from her.

Often she had asked herself the painful questions, *What have I done wrong?* and, *Why is God not merciful to me—why doesn't He bless me with children?*

She was now very old, and the much-desired child had not come.[5] Was she still expectant, even at this age? Or had

---

[4] Luke 1:6
[5] Luke 1:7

she resigned herself to the thought that her prayers were not pleasing to the Lord and that she would have no children?

Do you remain expectant for answers to prayers? Which Scriptures help you battle discouragement when God seems silent?

Did she draw courage from the lives of Sarah, Rebekah, and Hannah—women who also had been without children for a long time?

Life was full of surprises, not only for the mothers of Isaac, Jacob, and Samuel—women who after waiting so many years finally had great sons—but also for Elizabeth.

Her husband belonged to a group of priests who served in the house of the Lord.[6] During his period of duty, Zechariah had the opportunity to burn incense in the sanctuary. This was a great honor, one that a priest could receive, at most, once in his life. Many never received it. The day Zechariah burned the incense opened up a new phase of life for him and Elizabeth. As so often is the case when heaven seems silent for a long time, everything happened at once.

Gabriel, God's special messenger, stood before the priest and said, "Do not be afraid, Zechariah; your prayer has been heard. Your wife Elizabeth will bear you a son, and you are to call him John."[7]

[6] 1 Chronicles 24:6-19; Luke 1:5
[7] Luke 1:13, NIV

The long wait was being rewarded. Zechariah and Elizabeth would have a son. God was going to remove their shame. New life was coming into their quiet home. Quietness would be banished by the tramping of the child's feet and his shouting laughter. But God had still more good news.

A new future was dawning for the entire nation!

Their son would not be like every other child. He would be a man dedicated to God who would help his people return to God.[8] Jesus would testify of him that no greater man had ever lived.[9]

The horizon widened; the vision increased. The blessing that was to result from the birth of John would stretch far beyond the small borders of his own country and people. It would reach out to the entire world. John would be the man to prepare the way for the coming Messiah. He was the herald of the kingdom to come.

"Zechariah, your prayers have indeed been heard. Not only your prayers regarding a child, but also your prayers regarding the Messiah."

How could a human being embrace so much happiness at once?

Read Ephesians 3:20-21. Has God ever answered a prayer beyond anything you could have imagined? How did you respond?

---

[8] Luke 1:14-16
[9] Matthew 11:11

Zechariah revealed that he couldn't. He asked for a sign, and God gave him His answer. For nine full months he could not utter a word.[10] Everything he desired to say he had to write down.

But Elizabeth evidently had no problems in believing the fantastic promise, even though she had not received it as her husband had, directly from God through a godly messenger. She had to accept it prosaically as her husband wrote it down.

Did Elizabeth have such a close walk with God that she could hear His voice? Or had she responded more in faith? The Bible doesn't say.

If you had been in Elizabeth's situation, would it have been hard for you to respond in faith? Why do you think her response was so different from that of Sarah, who was in a similar situation centuries earlier?

While many people in the West simply choose a baby's name for the way it sounds or name him after a special friend, this was not true in Elizabeth's society. John's name was like a clarion call: "God is gracious!" God Himself gave this name to John. No one could have given him a more beautiful one.

Elizabeth was thinking about these things while the miracle took place within her body. She withdrew for five

---
[10] Luke 1:18-20

months. Was it because she felt ill at ease showing her growing body to the inquisitive people around her? Perhaps.

But her main reason was God. She marveled at the miracle
that was taking place—not only because God had proved
again that He specializes in the impossible, but also because
of His unending faithfulness.

---

*When God places His hand of blessing upon
you, do you take time to rest in it, cultivating
a spirit of thankfulness by dwelling in His
presence? What could you do to withdraw
from your busy context and spend time
reflecting on His blessings in your life?*

What had seemed to be a punishment now proved to be
a blessing.

God had a very special son in mind for her and Zechariah,
but they had to wait for His timing. John couldn't be born
until the birth of the Lord Jesus was at hand. She was going
to bring an exceptional child into the world, a child who
would have a unique place in history. She was blessed indeed.

---

*Think of a time when you had to wait on God's
timing. What did you learn about Him during
that time? How did you grow in your faith?*

Her patience had been greatly tested and was exceptionally rewarded.

If Elizabeth did react more spiritually than her husband to the news, there is no evidence of any self-exaltation. Nor did she look down on him. She didn't move him down in order to move herself up. Rather, she responded like a good wife who accepts weakness in her life partner.

Not only did Elizabeth have a distinguished background, but she also had a distinguished and independent character, in the positive sense of this word. When their son was born, the relatives and neighbors interfered—trying to force the tradition of giving the child his father's name.

Elizabeth refused this choice.[11]

She would not give in to conforming pressure but remained loyal to her husband and to God. Firmly and resolutely, she said, "His name will be John."

Her life was characterized by other virtues, such as humility and modesty. These were evident in an outstanding way when her relative Mary visited her unexpectedly during her pregnancy.[12] Rivalry was totally foreign to Elizabeth.[13]

Rather than talk about herself, she gave all her attention to Mary, whom she recognized at once as her superior. It became a meeting, not of an old woman and a young one, but of the mother of John—the preparer of the way—with the mother of Immanuel, the Messiah, whose way must be prepared. That made a big difference. Elizabeth acknowledged

[11] Luke 1:57-59
[12] Luke 1:39-40
[13] 1 Corinthians 10:24

this with a humility and modesty one could be envious of. She was not jealous in the least. She didn't find it difficult to call the much younger woman "the mother of my Lord" and blessed among women.[14]

This was the work of the Holy Spirit in her. The ninefold fruit of the Spirit that Paul listed later[15] was already present in her. Even before Mary was able to share her great happiness, Elizabeth knew what was happening. Elizabeth saw—so to speak—the unborn child and worshiped Him as her Lord. The other unborn child—the one in her—leaped with joy, as if he wanted to welcome his Master, the One he would humbly serve later on.[16]

Study Elizabeth's life in light of Galatians 5:22-23. Which aspects of the fruit of the Spirit do you see in her life? (Also read Philippians 2:3-4 and 1 Corinthians 10:24.) Cite specific actions or words that illustrate those fruits.

At that moment, the woman who had been reproached for her childlessness became a prophetess. "Blessed is she who has believed that the Lord would fulfill his promises to her!"[17] she said.

---

[14] Luke 1:42-43
[15] Galatians 5:22-23
[16] John 3:30
[17] Luke 1:45

For three months the mothers-to-be remained together—women who were writing history.[18]

They talked a lot and laughed a lot, but uppermost in their minds was what God was going to do. Luke is very clear about this. It was no wonder that all the people in the hill country of Judea who lived near them talked about John and his parents. People took what was happening to heart and said, "Watch that child. Wait and see what will become of him. God's hand is upon him in a special way."[19]

A new expectation broke loose. People began looking forward to what God was going to do. They were prepared for great things to come, for the Man who would come—Jesus, the Messiah—and for the man who would prepare His way—John the Baptist. For all of this God used Elizabeth, a woman of faith and remarkable character. What made her remarkable was that she was full of God.

God can use such a woman to accomplish marvelous things.

What expectations do you have of the great work of God? How might He use you to accomplish His purposes?

---

[18] Luke 1:56
[19] Luke 1:65-66, author's paraphrase

8

ANNA

A Woman Who Wasn't Destroyed by a Broken Heart

[Anna] permitted her heartbreak to force her to God. . . .
Those of us who have faced tragedy of any kind—particularly
those of you who are widows—*know* that nothing heals the
wounds like being consciously with God.

EUGENIA PRICE, *THE UNIQUE WORLD OF WOMEN*

READ

Jeremiah 49:11; Psalm 147:3; Luke 2:22-27,36-38

• • •

CAN A PERSON DIE OF A BROKEN HEART?

British medical doctors, studying the cases of a large group
of widowers, discovered that a number of them died within
the first six months after the deaths of their wives—50 percent
of them through heart failure.

The prophetess Anna's life should have been without
hope. The only thing a childless woman in Anna's time could
do after the death of her husband was return to the house of
her parents to wait for a second husband or death.

The happiness of Anna's marriage lasted only seven years.[1]

---

[1] Luke 2:36

Bible commentators say that she had been a widow for over sixty years. She was a prophetess out of the tribe of Asher from Galilee, of which it had been said that "a prophet does not come out of Galilee."[2]

Do you ever feel insignificant because of your background, job, or relationships? How might Anna's story encourage you?

Prophets were usually men. A female prophet was rare. The Bible names a few: Miriam, Deborah, Huldah, and Noadiah in the Old Testament, and the four daughters of Philip the evangelist in the New Testament.[3]

Anna stands between the Old and the New Testaments.

It was an honor to be a prophetess. Like a male prophet, a woman who spoke the Word of God to the people was exceptionally privileged. Anna belonged to a select group.

How does the Bible describe Anna's relationship with God? What conclusions do you draw from this?

Relational loneliness exists in many forms in our lives. Some women watch the people around them find spouses and start families and wonder when their turn will come.

[2] John 7:52
[3] Exodus 15:20; Judges 4:4; 2 Kings 22:14; Nehemiah 6:14; Acts 21:8-9

Others lose a spouse through death or divorce and feel a gaping hole in the middle of their lives. Some women, though married, feel estranged and distant from their spouses and very much alone. In each of these situations, the temptation can be to feel as though life stops in the face of a relational void. But Anna took a completely different point of view. She didn't flee to isolation and self-pity after the great blow in her life. She didn't become a burden to her relatives. She didn't become a lonely woman to whom life had nothing to offer, nor did she become a person whom everyone pitied but no one knew how to help. And she didn't flee into the past or retreat to daydreams of an imagined future. Each of these roads is a serious threat to a healthy spiritual life.

In cases of death, divorce, or distance, when the unity of a married couple is broken, what remains is a single person torn in two. Even after a relatively short marriage, the one who remains behind is never the same as he or she was before. The person remains half of two people. Similarly, those struggling with being single feel as though a piece of them remains just out of reach.

Was Anna comforted by the thought that God doesn't just take for the sake of taking away? Did she expect that He would give Himself in exchange for what He took from her? Most likely. A person must have courage and farsightedness to embrace that attitude. Jesus later told His disciples that no one who put his hand to the plow and looked back was fit for the kingdom of God.[4]

---

[4] Luke 9:62

*How has God given Himself in exchange
for something you have lost in your life?*

Anna didn't flee to memories of the past or dreams of the future. She fled to God. She dedicated her life to serving Him in His temple. She prayed and fasted. She was willing to give more attention to God than to herself and to give His work the highest priority.

When a woman dares to leave the past and future alone, when she is not dependent upon memories or dreams for true happiness, and when she dares to face both now and what is to come with God, a supernatural peace floods her heart. She no longer stands in life as one bereft, but as one who comforts. She can comfort others in problems and mourning because she herself has been comforted by God.[5]

*If you struggle with relational loneliness,
whether through singleness, loss of a spouse,
or a marriage filled with emotional distance,
how has God comforted you? Have you
considered expanding a ministry of comfort
to others as a response to His comfort?
If you don't feel that He has brought you
comfort, what other things might you be
fleeing to that are a barrier to His comfort?*

[5] 2 Corinthians 1:3-4

Anna was occupied with God's work not only during the day, but also during the night.[6] Yet despite all her activities, she didn't lose sight of people. A real walk with God isn't only introspective; it is also outgoing. It wants to make others happy. Søren Kierkegaard once said, "The door of happiness opens to the outside . . . to others."

The world was dark, gloomy, and without hope in Anna's day. The problems had become too great for the people to bear. Many, therefore, were looking consciously or subconsciously for a redemption that could only come from God—the coming of the Messiah.

Who in your life is weighed down with trouble? How can you share with them the redemption that comes from God?

Suddenly, the great day had come. Jesus was born!

When Joseph and Mary took their firstborn to the temple to present Him to God as required by the Law, they not only found the pious Simeon there—the man who knew he wouldn't die before seeing the Messiah[7]—but they also encountered Anna. God, who had cared for her so faithfully all these years, saw to it that she didn't miss that sacred moment. The woman who wouldn't have ordinarily had any chance in life—because of her background, widowed status, and age—at that moment became one of the most privileged

---

[6] Luke 2:37
[7] Luke 2:26

women in the world. Together with Simeon, she was allowed to see the child and worship Him.

This was the crowning moment of her life, the answer to the prayers of many years. This was the greatest moment of all ages, the moment the world had been waiting for so anxiously—the Messiah had come!

It was only natural for Anna to do two things. First, she joined Simeon in praising and worshiping God because the long-expected Redeemer of her people, of the world, and of her own sins, had come. Second, she decided she couldn't possibly keep this exciting news to herself. Someone has said, "Witnessing is taking a good look at the Lord Jesus Christ and then telling others what you have seen." This was Anna's response.

Do you keep the good news about Jesus to yourself? What would it look like for this news to overflow in your life?

This proves how well she knew people. She knew all those in Jerusalem who were looking forward to the Savior. She went and told these people what she had seen.

This proclaimer of Jesus Christ was not an energetic young man of eloquent speech, but an old woman. She was someone who had experienced what the psalmist had written about the Lord: "He heals the brokenhearted and binds up their wounds."[8]

---

[8] Psalm 147:3

9

THE POOR WIDOW

A Woman Who Handled Money with Faith

I will place no value on anything I have or may possess, except in relation to the kingdom of Christ. If anything will advance the interests of that kingdom, it shall be given away or kept, only as by giving or keeping of it I shall most promote the glory of Him to whom I owe all my hopes in time and eternity.

DAVID LIVINGSTONE

READ

Mark 12:41-44; 2 Corinthians 9:6-8

• • •

JERUSALEM WAS BUSY. Jews from all over the known world were flocking to the city. It would soon be Passover, and every devout Jew wanted to celebrate the festival days in the Holy City.[1]

At home, the women were busily preparing the Passover meal. They had bought great quantities of food to cook and bake for the great feasts.

But one woman was not joining the festivities. She hadn't spent her money on food because she didn't have much and, therefore, had to spend it wisely. She didn't earn much

---

[1] Mark 14:1

money—but she did know exactly what to do with what she had. She walked straight to the temple, and there, without any hesitation, she put her two tiny copper coins into the treasury box. Rich men jostled past her and threw great quantities of money into the box—money from their abundance.[2] Then she withdrew as inconspicuously as she had come.

Inconspicuously?

Not as far as Jesus was concerned. He was in the temple. His visits to His Father's house were numbered. In a few more days He would be taken captive in a garden. He would then be crucified. Important things were about to happen. In fact, the most significant act of history was about to occur. Yet He had time to notice a poor widow give God her two pennies.

He stood watching people toss money into the treasury box. He saw the rich give a lot, and that was good. But their gifts hardly made a dent in their abundant possessions. They had so much left over. Then the poor widow came. Jesus knew what she was doing. He knew that the two coins were the last ones she possessed. She had literally given her entire worldly wealth to the God she loved. The pennies wouldn't reach far in paying the bills of the temple—what could one buy for two pennies?

Is giving an important part of your relationship with God? Do you give out of your abundance, or is your giving a sacrificial act?

---

[2] Mark 12:41-42

But Jesus thought her gift was so important that He drew His disciples' attention to it. He said, "This poor widow has put more into the treasury than all the others. They all gave out of their wealth; but she, out of her poverty, put in every-thing—all she had to live on."[3] To the Lord, how much she gave was not as important as how much she still had after giving. She had nothing left. Jesus was concerned with what the money represented to the giver. To this woman it repre-sented everything.

What does money represent to you?
How does your attitude toward
money influence your actions?

Money itself has no value to God. Paul wrote, "The God who made the world and everything in it is the Lord of heaven and earth and does not live in temples built by human hands. And he is not served by human hands, as if he needed anything. Rather, he himself gives everyone life and breath and everything else."[4]

God is interested in the motives of the person who gives. He knows that, by nature, people tend to hold their money closely. They often forget that only by God's grace can they earn money, since He gives health and a sound mind.[5] They often mistakenly think, *I can do what I like with my money.*

[3] Mark 12:43-44
[4] Acts 17:24,25
[5] Proverbs 10:22; 2 Timothy 1:7, PH

God does not desire for people to give because He needs it. He only wants them to use their money in the right way. He knows that when people give sacrificially to God, they do so because they love Him—because they want to share all, even their possessions, with Him. Then He multiplies the actual value of the money, as He multiplied the loaves and the fish.[6] He can perform miracles with it. Those who share all with God will discover that much can be done with little when God adds His blessing.

Do you believe that God can multiply the money you give to Him? What might that look like?

It is remarkable that this poor widow sensed the atmosphere of New Testament giving while she still lived under the Old Testament covenant, where giving was governed by law. Under the old covenant, God gave precise rules for giving money—10 percent of all income for His purposes.[7] From this percentage the temple servants, the Levites, were paid. No Israelite could escape this obligation. Even the Levites had to, in turn, give 10 percent of their money.[8]

But in the New Testament, the situation is different. There are no stiff regulations, no set amounts. The motivating factor is love instead of law. And love cannot be regulated by law. It has to be a voluntary expression. Those who are

[6] Luke 9:12-17
[7] Leviticus 27:30,32
[8] Numbers 18:21,25-30

guided by this principle have pleasure in giving. They give regularly.[9] They give unobtrusively.[10]

Examine your heart motivations in your giving. Do you give out of obligation? Habit? How might you begin practicing an attitude of love when you give?

Did this woman sense that God was about to give His Son to the world? The greatest single act of love? Was this the reason she wanted to prove her love to Him by her total dedication? She understood that giving was not the exclusive privilege of the rich. Poor people have the same opportunity. The percentage that the poor can give of their wages is no smaller than the percentage the rich can give. While the actual amount may be smaller, the percentage remains the same.

Money has exciting potential when dedicated to God and His service, because then it has lasting value. "Money," someone once said, "is something you cannot take with you to heaven, but you can send it on ahead." It can be used for transactions of eternal value, as the widow's was. Money then becomes a capital investment in heaven.[11]

It is a pity that the veil covering this woman's life was lifted only slightly. It would be interesting to know how He, who was touched by her sacrificial gift, took care of her. Didn't He

---

[9] 1 Corinthians 16:2
[10] Matthew 6:2-4
[11] Philippians 4:17

say through Solomon, "Honor the LORD with your wealth, with the firstfruits of all your crops; then your barns will be filled to overflowing, and your vats will brim over with new wine."[12] And through the mouth of Malachi hadn't He promised showerings of blessings to the person who gave just 10 percent of his income?[13] The poor widow had not been satisfied to give only a part of her money. Ten percent was too small an act of devotion to God. She wanted to give 100 percent. Since God doesn't want to be any man's debtor, there are no limitations to the blessings He could have bestowed upon this poor woman.

One thing is certain—she celebrated a wonderful Passover.

God honors obedience. Blessings from Him come in many forms. How is He blessing your life right now?

---

[12] Proverbs 3:9-10
[13] Malachi 3:10

10

MARY OF JERUSALEM

A Woman Whose Home Functioned as the House of God

I pray Heaven to bestow The best of Blessings on this House and on all that shall hereafter inhabit it. May none but honest and wise Men ever rule under this roof.

JOHN ADAMS

READ

Acts 12:1-17

$$\bullet \quad \bullet \quad \bullet$$

THE NIGHT HAD LONG SINCE FALLEN OVER JERUSALEM. The houses of Israel's capital city were completely dark, for the oil lamps had been put out some hours ago.

Yet in the house of Mary, all the lamps burned brightly. But no one could see light from the outside, so carefully had the windows been covered. Not even a small ray of light peeped out. People on the street were kept from knowing what was going on inside the home.

Were the people in the house doing something so bad that it could not stand to be exposed to the light? Not at all.

The people in Mary's house were Christians, followers of Jesus Christ. They had been meeting together in this house for some time.

These Christians formed a minority group. Such a heavy persecution of believers had broken out that many had fled outside Jerusalem.[1] Those who stayed behind were constantly in danger. The threat of arrest and prison hung over their heads.

"My house is spacious enough," Mary said. "Why don't we have the meetings at my place? My home can easily function as a church building."

Mary didn't seem worried about her own life. Because she loved God, she accepted matter-of-factly that the coming and going of many people meant work, expense, and inconvenience.

Thus Mary of Jerusalem revealed herself as a courageous and sacrificial woman. In some ways she resembled Martha and Mary, who during a time when Jewish leaders were trying to kill Jesus[2] were not afraid to meet with Him. She was an indispensable link in the chain of life in the early church.

In which way did Mary follow the examples of other women who served Christ (Luke 8:1-3)? List and summarize the contributions of other women in the Bible who placed their homes at the disposal of God (see 1 Kings 17:10-22; 2 Kings 4:8-11).

---

[1] Acts 8:1
[2] John 11:54-57; 12:1-11

In Scripture, her house is called "the house of Mary."[3] Had Mary's husband died? Was she therefore more drawn toward God? Was she aware of the fact that in the past He had proven Himself strong toward widows who trusted Him?

Wasn't the prophet Elijah kept alive during famine by a widow?[4] Wasn't the prophetess Anna—the first woman privileged to see the child Jesus in the temple[5] and one who heralded His entrance into Jerusalem—also a widow?

God often powerfully uses those the world might see as weak—in this case, a woman without a husband in a society ruled by men. How does God's consistent honoring and empowerment of women speak to your heart?

The reason that Christians were together this night and hadn't gone home at the usual time stemmed from an emergency. They were in great trouble. King Herod Agrippa had arrested Peter.[6]

The Jewish leaders, jealous because of the signs and miracles the apostles were performing, had put believers in prison before.[7] And though God Himself, by means of an angel, had delivered His servants from prison, the opposition remained. Stephen's blood had been shed,[8] and the people desired more.

---

[3] Acts 12:12
[4] 1 Kings 17:7-16
[5] Luke 2:25-38
[6] Acts 12:1-3
[7] Acts 5:17-20
[8] Acts 7:57-60

No good could be expected from Herod. The hatred against Jesus and His followers permeated the family of this ruler. Hadn't his grandfather, Herod the Great, forever entered history as the man who murdered the children in Bethlehem?[9] And hadn't this Herod's predecessor, Herod Antipas, beheaded John the Baptist?[10] Herod Agrippa himself had recently killed James, the brother of John and a disciple of Jesus.[11]

There was no doubt that Peter would also die, probably in public. Then everybody would see what the king thought about the followers of Jesus.

The believers gathered together to pray on the night that seemed to be the last one of Peter's earthly life.

Peter, meanwhile, was sound asleep, despite being locked up in the prison with chains on his hands. He was not lying awake from fear, wondering what might happen to him the next day. The sixteen soldiers who guarded him in groups of four were not keeping him from his sleep.[12]

Interrupted sleep is often a doorway for anxious thoughts. How can you combat fear with faith when anxiety begins to creep in?

Yet no human being would be able to deliver him. He was completely locked away from the outside world. An impassable wall stood between him and freedom. The guards

---

[9] Matthew 2:16
[10] Matthew 14:1-12
[11] Acts 12:1-2
[12] Acts 12:4,6

guaranteed that he could not break out. "But the church was earnestly praying to God for him."[13] Although the way out might be totally closed, the way up remained open.

In times of trouble, do you turn to faithful friends for prayer?

Herod Agrippa wanted to make sure that Peter's friends could not liberate the apostle. But those friends, though having no might in themselves, through prayer had a weapon against which King Herod had no power.

Christ had given many promises in connection with prayer before His ascension. "Again, truly I tell you that if two of you on earth agree about anything they ask for, it will be done for them by my Father in heaven."[14] He had also promised that "where two or three gather in my name, there am I with them."[15]

"You can get anything—*anything* you ask for in prayer," Jesus had said, "if you believe."[16]

Another time, Christ illustrated His challenge not to slow down in prayer with the example of a widow who continued to ask—and eventually received what she asked for.[17]

The disciples knew that these promises hadn't lost their power. They were still valid, even though Jesus was no longer on earth with them. They knew that He supported their

---

[13] Acts 12:5
[14] Matthew 18:19
[15] Matthew 18:20
[16] Matthew 21:22, author's paraphrase
[17] Luke 18:1-8

prayers from heaven, that He was interceding for them,[18] and that He would answer them.

_____

Do you believe Jesus' promises about prayer?
Have you faced times when you feel as
though your prayers fall on deaf ears?
Based on your knowledge of Scripture, how
might God still be fulfilling His promises
(or fulfill His promises in the future)?

_____

The Christians who met in Mary's house believed that the prayers of righteous people had great power and would have wonderful results.[19] Thus it happened that while they were, after the words of the prophet Isaiah, leaving God no rest,[20] He answered. A supernatural messenger, an angel, descended into Peter's prison. The darkness of the night vanished when he arrived. Iron chains broke and dropped to the ground.

After the angel had released Peter's chains, he led him outside, unhindered by closed doors. He made the guards deaf and blind, and they did not notice what was happening. Peter, roused from his sleep, experienced what was happening like a dream. In a few moments he stood outside, not knowing whether he was awake or asleep.[21]

While the believers naturally were ignorant of what was

---

[18] Hebrews 7:25
[19] James 5:16
[20] Isaiah 62:7
[21] Acts 12:7-9

happening, Peter was passing through the gate into Jerusalem. Eventually he realized that he was not dreaming. Thankful to God for his freedom, he headed straight for the home of Mary.[22]

How would you have felt if Peter had come to the door for shelter during a time of persecution of Christians? In your opinion, which of Mary's characteristics gave her the strength to risk possible imprisonment or even death?

The believers experienced the truth of what God had said centuries ago through the mouth of Isaiah: "I will answer them before they even call to me. While they are still talking about their needs, I will go ahead and answer their prayers!"[23]

Has God ever come to your aid even before you had a chance to ask Him to? If so, what did you learn about Him through that experience?

After the Holy Spirit came down on the Day of Pentecost, many Christians sold their houses or properties and offered the proceeds to other needy believers.

Mary had not done that. She did not sell her spacious

---

[22] Acts 12:10-12
[23] Isaiah 65:24, NLT

home and give away the proceeds. Instead, she kept her house but placed it at the disposal of the church.

In light of Matthew 18:19-20, how might your home be used for the glory of God and the care of His church?

Mary was an independent woman led by God in an individual way. She realized that there were different ways to serve God. She could serve God and her fellow believers with the money she received from selling her possessions. But she could also serve God—as He had led her—by sharing the possession itself with those in need.

Mary understood that the gifts the Holy Spirit distributed among Christians differed. The church of Christ was like a mosaic, for it contained many forms and many colors.

Mary continued the tradition of the women who had lived close to Christ, supporting Him with their private means.[24] She occupied her own place in the mosaic of the church. Her task was as important as those of people who in the eyes of the public seemed to be more prominent. Her influence in the church was undeniable, irreplaceable. God made Peter's travels to preach the gospel and his opportunity to work miracles again[25] partially dependent on people like Mary of Jerusalem. Mary had her function within the church.

---

[24] Luke 8:3
[25] Acts 3:6-8; 5:15

What are your spiritual gifts? How has God empowered you practically to take your place in the mosaic of the church?

But that was not all of her responsibility. She also was the mother of John Mark.[26] As a mother, Mary experienced the joy of knowing that her son was serving the Lord. Not only did her life influence outsiders—it also affected her own son. Did God reward the mother through the opportunities He was giving to the son?

John Mark received the exceptional privilege of becoming the helper of Paul and Barnabas.[27] Later he became the traveling companion of Peter, who lovingly called him "my son."[28] What the fellowship with these three great men in the kingdom of God meant for Mark and how it influenced his character can easily be imagined.

The Bible mentions Mary's name only once, and the emphasis is not on her but on her home. According to a legend, this is the same home in whose upper room Jesus celebrated the Last Supper with His disciples.

The rest of Mary's life is veiled. But one day, God's "scroll of remembrance"—the book in which He records the deeds of men and women[29]—will be opened. Only then will it become clear what Mary has meant to the kingdom of God.

---

[26] Acts 12:12
[27] Acts 12:25; 13:5
[28] 1 Peter 5:13
[29] Malachi 3:16

What unnoticed work are you doing for the kingdom of God? Be encouraged that work done for His glory alone will be honored in heaven.

Until that time she will continue to be an example to every woman. She showed what a tremendous influence a godly woman who puts her home at the disposal of God can have.

11

TABITHA

A Woman Who Loved God

When a young woman really accepts her not being married, then this means such a liberation to her that in her unmarried situation she can make her special feminine characteristics useful to the most.

DR. PAUL TOURNIER, *THE HEALING OF PERSONS*

READ

Acts 9:36-42; Romans 12:4-8; James 1:27

• • •

TABITHA WAS NOT A PARTICULARLY STRIKING WOMAN. She could sew well, but who would call that remarkable?[1] Many women could do as much.

Tabitha was a woman whose talent was an inconspicuous one.[2] It would have been easy for Tabitha to think, *I am no prophetess like Miriam, and I cannot rule a country like Deborah. I am not a woman who will play a large role in the history of my country. I don't belong in the category of gifted women.*

---
[1] Acts 9:39
[2] Matthew 25:14-29

*Do you ever feel as though what you have
to offer is insignificant? In what ways
might God want to use your gifts?*

It seems that marriage and motherhood had also bypassed her. Otherwise, she could have indirectly influenced society through her husband or son. Wasn't it true that in the history of her country, the destiny of a king of Israel had often been guided by his mother?[3]

Yet there is one thing in which Tabitha surpassed every other woman in the Bible. She is the only one who was called a disciple![4] Tabitha was a disciple, a follower of Jesus, and that changed everything.

*What is the definition of a disciple?
What does being a disciple look like in your life?*

She opened her heart to Him before she followed Him. He became her Savior before He became her Lord. And although she had received Him as her Redeemer, she didn't stop there. Faith is more than just fellowship with God. One uses it to serve others—true faith expresses itself in deeds. A person who follows Christ is moved toward people as He

[3] 1 Kings 1:11-31
[4] Acts 9:36

was. She becomes creative and wants to do all she can to give her life maximum purpose. Therefore, the disciple Tabitha did what came naturally to her. She sewed, especially for the poor widows. She sewed to the best of her ability.

Joppa (now Jaffa), a port along the Mediterranean Sea, must have had a large population of widows. During the season of bad weather, many of its fishermen were shipwrecked and drowned. These women had lost not only their husbands but also their incomes. There was no government assistance in those days, but that really wasn't necessary, for again and again, God had told His people to take good care of widows and orphans.[5] If the people obeyed God's orders, then the widows had no needs and the people enjoyed abundant blessing as the reward that God had promised them.[6]

Who are the widows and orphans in your life? They may not be literal widows or orphans, but people who are struggling to get by. How can you and your church care for these people?

God had promised that He would be husband to the widows.[7] They enjoyed His special protection and care. Being a disciple, Tabitha knew what made her Lord happy, and that was to take care of this group of people in whom He was interested in a special way. Therefore, she didn't do her work

[5] Exodus 22:22-24; Deuteronomy 10:17-18
[6] Deuteronomy 14:29; 24:19
[7] Isaiah 54:4-5

halfheartedly. It wasn't just a pastime to her. She did it with a definite goal in mind. She did it with all her heart because she loved God. When Jesus had entered her heart, Tabitha had become a free woman. He had called Himself the Truth.[8] He stated further that those who were freed by Him are *truly* free.[9] Tabitha operated from this base of freedom.

Do you view your work, no matter what it is, as a calling from God? Does your love for God drive how you approach your work?

The Bible leaves room for the thought that Tabitha was an unmarried woman, but this does not seem to have caused her to be frustrated by feelings of inferiority. She had no desire to compete in importance with the married women around her. She was not jealous of mothers with children.

Do you feel a sense of competition with women who are in different life stages, jobs, or relationships? How might your attitude toward other women hinder your faith?

Tabitha became a woman who was far ahead of her time. She experienced fulfillment while working at a profession

[8] John 14:6
[9] John 8:32,36

of her own, which was unique for the time in which she lived. Tabitha met a real need by sewing. She required little for herself. She lived for others. That was the reason for her happiness.

Many of the widows in Joppa were walking around in clothing sewn by Tabitha. There was a growing gratitude toward her. Tabitha, who probably stood alone in life, was able to give moral and spiritual support to the widows. She understood lonely women and could talk with them. Consequently, she utilized her potential. In so doing, she became a person of importance in the church. But then came a sudden blow—Tabitha became ill and died.[10]

Someone remembered that Peter was working in Lydda, only ten miles away, and hastily sent two men to fetch him.[11] They knew that he possessed supernatural power. Hadn't they heard that sick people were restored when Peter's shadow fell on them?[12] Hadn't he and John healed a lame man?[13] All their hopes were centered on him. Peter came right away. In the upper room where the dead body lay, weeping women encircled Peter. They told him how terribly they missed Tabitha, how bereft they were without her. They showed him the clothes she had made for them.[14]

Often only good things are said of the dead. In this case, however, it was very obvious how those who stayed behind were suffering from the loss of the life that had been taken.

[10] Acts 9:37
[11] Acts 9:38
[12] Acts 5:15
[13] Acts 3:1–10
[14] Acts 9:39

Tabitha's love for them had given them a great love for her. What else could be expected? Peter did what he saw the Lord do in a similar situation.[15] He asked everyone to leave the room. Then he prayed and restored Tabitha to life through the power of God.[16]

How do you practically love those around you well? What can you do to show increasing love to those around you?

The Bible records accounts of seven people who were raised from the dead. Tabitha was the only adult woman among them. The news of her resurrection became the talk of the day in Joppa. "Did you hear?" the people exclaimed to one another. "Tabitha is alive again! Peter has raised her from the dead."[17]

Then something else remarkable occurred. The people realized that God had worked a miracle, so they honored God Himself rather than Tabitha or Peter. Through these happenings, people realized the emptiness of their own lives. They also desired to believe in the Lord Jesus. They began to understand some of the real values in life. They wanted to belong to Him as Tabitha did. They desired to become Christians, new people with a new perspective on life.

[15] Mark 5:40-42
[16] Acts 9:40
[17] Acts 9:41-42

Do you serve others in such a way that points them toward Jesus? How can you tell people about the good news through your actions?

Long ago, the Lord had asked Moses, "What is that in your hand?"

Moses answered, "A rod."

"Go and work with that rod," God said, "and you will be My servant."[18]

If God had asked Tabitha the same question, she would have answered, "A needle and thread, Lord." Then He would have shown her that these were precisely the instruments with which she could serve Him.

How would you answer God's question to Moses? How can your answer inform how you serve God?

The life, death, and resurrection of Tabitha helped spread the gospel. Peter could not leave Joppa for a while because the people who were inquiring about God needed him.[19]

Tabitha started a movement that spread beyond the borders of her city and country. Indirectly she became a great evangelist. Today there are organizations all over the world

---

[18] Exodus 4:2-5, author's paraphrase
[19] Acts 9:43

that are feeding and clothing needy people in the name of Christ, just as Tabitha did.

Who can number the countless women who were influenced by the life of this woman, Tabitha? Her bright example will never be extinguished. That is the most any disciple can desire.

12

LOIS AND EUNICE

Women Who Were Convinced of the Power of God's Word

The Lord Jesus was a living reality to me. In the time I was still very young my mother told me how dearly He loved children and how He wanted to live in their hearts. I must have asked Him to come in, though I don't know how and when.

CORRIE TEN BOOM, *IN HEM GEBORGEN*

READ

2 Timothy 1:5; 2 Timothy 3:14-17; Acts 16:1-3

• • •

THE NAMES OF LOIS AND EUNICE CANNOT BE SEPARATED. This is not simply because they were mother and daughter, but because they exhibited sincere faith and a high regard for the Holy Scriptures. Most important of all, though, they had mutual interest in Timothy, the son of Eunice and the grandson of Lois.

Their names occur only once in the Bible. But one must not, from that fact alone, jump to the conclusion that their lives were unimportant or that their influence was relatively small. The opposite is true. Their names are forever written down in history because of the indelible impression they made on the apostle Paul, one of the greatest evangelists and the writer of much of the New Testament, including two letters to Timothy.

Does generational faith exist in your family? If not, what are you doing to create generational faith in your life? Generational faith doesn't have to include blood relatives—just as Paul mentored Timothy, we can create spiritual generations with anyone God places in our path.

Around AD 67, Paul included these words in his last letter to Timothy from Rome: "I am reminded of your sincere faith," he wrote, "which first lived in your grandmother Lois and in your mother Eunice and, I am persuaded, now lives in you also."[1]

The persecution of Christians had begun during Emperor Nero's reign some years before and had culminated in a terrible fire that the emperor started himself but for which he blamed the Christians. That way he gave himself an excuse to persecute them.

Tradition states that Paul fell victim to that persecution. Imprisoned in Rome and waiting for his death, he wrote to his "dear son," Timothy.[2] He was looking forward with great

[1] 2 Timothy 1:5
[2] 2 Timothy 1:2, NLT

desire to seeing his faithful and beloved colaborer one last time.[3]

Paul knew that his earthly life was almost finished. His service was nearly completed.[4] But through Timothy (and others), the work he had started would continue. In this letter, the man who had accompanied him on so many trips—the colaborer he had sent to different churches—would receive final instructions from his leader and teacher. These instructions would help Timothy to execute the task he and others were taking over from Paul.[5]

What work are you doing for the kingdom?
Who are your partners in that work?

The reason Paul could write that he had fought the good fight and was living in the expectation of receiving the crown of righteousness[6] also had to do with Timothy.

Paul was convinced that the spiritual education and help he had given Timothy would not stop there, for Timothy had already proven that he took the lessons he had learned to heart. Once again Paul directed him toward the tasks that lay ahead. "And the things you have heard me say in the presence of many witnesses entrust to reliable people who will also be qualified to teach others,"[7] Paul wrote.

---

[3] 2 Timothy 4:9
[4] 2 Timothy 4:6
[5] 2 Timothy 4:2
[6] 2 Timothy 4:7-8
[7] 2 Timothy 2:2

Who is a trustworthy woman in your life to whom you could pass on scriptural truths?

As far as Paul was concerned, that teaching had started about twenty years earlier in Lystra. There he had briefly met Timothy while he was preaching during what was probably his first visit to that part of the world.[8]

From the beginning, Paul had been struck by the boy's noble character and his God-fearing walk of life. Timothy, Paul found, had a good reputation with both the local Christians and those in nearby Iconium.[9] With proper training, he could become a useful instrument in the service of God, for he had been taught the Holy Scriptures since he was a small child. Shortly after Timothy's conversion to Christ, Paul began to look after him, carefully training him in the service of God.

How much time do you spend soaking in the Word? Does your study of Scripture influence your attitude and actions?

Timothy's initial instruction, however, had not started with Paul. Rather, it stemmed from the training begun years before under the direction of Lois and Eunice. Paul reaped what others had sown.

When the boy was born, his parents named him Timothy,

[8] Acts 14:6
[9] Acts 16:2

which meant "he that fears God." But that name probably was chosen more by his Jewish mother than by his Greek father.[10]

Why the God-fearing Eunice married a heathen man remains a secret. It is not known whether this happened with or without Lois's consent. Maybe both women were not Christians at that time. But whatever the case, Eunice's husband hadn't personally encountered the God in whom she believed. Consequently, Timothy remained uncircumcised.

Did the father die at an early age? Is that why the boy's education had to be undertaken by the mother? Did Eunice, being a widow, have to earn a living and therefore turn her son's education over to his grandmother?

Timothy thus was trained in the Holy Scriptures. That instruction was an invaluable privilege for which he never could thank God enough. He owed his religious education to his mother and grandmother. From his earliest childhood, he had been taught the Word of God.[11]

What was your experience with Scripture when you were a child? How has that impacted your interaction with Scripture later in life?

Lois and Eunice didn't think, *Let's raise him "neutrally" and then later he can make his own decisions.* Nor did they reason, *He is still too young. Later, when he can understand things better, we will start training him in the Word.*

[10] Acts 16:3
[11] 2 Timothy 2:15

Lois and Eunice attached great value to the Bible themselves, and they took every opportunity to confront the boy early and thoroughly with it. And mother and grandmother did not simply instill theoretical knowledge in Timothy. Day after day they showed him through their own lives how faith had to be applied in practice. This helped determine his character.

Of course they could go no further in their instruction than their knowledge reached. Being Jewish women living in a foreign land, they probably didn't know more than the content of the Old Testament. The message that the expected Messiah had come in the person of Jesus of Nazareth and that He was offering forgiveness of sin was not entirely clear to them. The news that God had become available to everyone who believed in Christ was something that became known through the messages of Paul.

However deeply the faith of the mother and grandmother had penetrated the life of the boy, it didn't save him. He himself had to make a personal choice for Jesus Christ. Like Paul, he had to believe that Jesus Christ came into the world to save sinners.[12] He also had to accept that he was a sinner.

The future messenger of the gospel first had to believe the gospel himself. He had to believe that Jesus Christ died, was buried, and rose from the dead according to the Scriptures.[13] He had to turn his life over to Christ on a personal level.

---

[12] 1 Timothy 1:15; Acts 16:31
[13] 1 Corinthians 15:1-4

Do you ever find yourself relying more on your knowledge of Scripture and the Christian life than on your personal faith in Jesus Christ? How might you adjust your perspective to put knowledge in its proper place?

When Paul had arrived in Lystra years before, God proved the truth of Isaiah's prophecy—that His Word would not return empty; it would accomplish the work He purposed to do.[14] Timothy, the son of Eunice and the grandson of Lois, became the "son in the Lord" of Paul. The apostle became his father in Christ Jesus through the gospel.[15]

Through the Holy Spirit's power, the mother and the grandmother had sown that Word generously in the receptive heart of a young child, and this resulted in new birth after Paul's preaching.[16]

Did Lois and Eunice possibly plead with God concerning the words of the illustrious King Solomon, who had written, "Train up a child in the way he should go: and when he is old, he will not depart from it"?[17]

Timothy first became a Christian and then an active messenger of Jesus Christ, an ambassador for God.[18] He became a man who would tell people the good news of the gospel.[19] His life gained eternal value. He was a wise man who shone

---

[14] Isaiah 55:11
[15] 1 Corinthians 4:15,17
[16] 1 Peter 1:23
[17] Proverbs 22:6, KJV
[18] 2 Corinthians 5:20
[19] 2 Timothy 4:5

"like the brightness of the heavens," because he led "many to righteousness."[20]

According to 2 Timothy 3:16-17, how does Scripture prepare a person for God's service?

What mother—what grandmother—could expect richer fruit from her teaching? How intensely grateful this mother and grandmother must have been when Timothy began his task of preaching the gospel. By instructing Timothy in the laws of the Hebrews, Lois and Eunice did not merely lay a foundation for Timothy's conversion; they also prepared him for his life's work.

As Timothy grew older, what things did he do in the service of God? (You may want to go through passages in the New Testament and develop a character study of Timothy.)

When he, still only a lad, left Lystra with Paul to replace Paul's former colaborer Barnabas, a heavy task was waiting for him. He would make long trips that could have broken his weak constitution. He would become entangled in difficulties against which his sensitive and timid nature would hardly be equal.

---

[20] Daniel 12:3

Every day of his life, Timothy would need the Word of God, which Lois and Eunice had given him. He would have to stick to it, live by it, and use it as a preparation for eternity. He could not do without it in everyday living. It was his comfort, his strength, his compass.

Do you view the Word of God as an integral part of how you face life? How do you use Scripture in your daily experiences?

In order to be a servant of God, up to his task and equipped to do good work, Timothy would take the Word for his guidance. He would be instructed and corrected by it. It would continue to educate him toward a godly character. The Word Timothy had learned to love and obey in the home would also inspire him and prove to be a necessary instrument in training others in biblical truth.

The link of faith from Lois to Eunice to Timothy didn't stop there. Through Timothy, many other people would come to embrace the same faith and would be stimulated and instructed to preach the gospel. He remained a colaborer with Paul till Paul's death, and the fact that Paul asked Timothy to come to Rome to comfort him in his last earthly hours shows the affection that bound them.[21]

Eunice and Lois naturally did not know the great plans God had for Timothy. Monica, likewise, did not know the

---

[21] 2 Timothy 4:9

role her son, Augustine, would play in church history. The mother of Billy Graham could not suspect how many people would become Christians through her son's ministry. God has wonderful surprises for mothers, grandmothers, and all of those who are trusting God to bless their loved ones.

If you are a mother, are you praying for how God might use your children for His glory? If you are not a mother, what children in your life could you commit to prayer?

How easily the lives of Lois and Eunice—two inconspicuous women who lived in Asia Minor (present-day Turkey)—could have remained anonymous.

Since they lived, the Bible has been translated into hundreds of languages, with millions of copies distributed. Until this day, Bible readers the world over continue to meet Lois and Eunice, two women who were convinced of the power of God's Word and its influence on a human life.

About the Author

GIEN KARSSEN was raised in a Christian home and became a Christian at the age of twelve as a result of the influence of her parents' lives and training. After she had been married only six weeks, the Nazis interned her husband in a concentration camp, where he died. Just before his death he inscribed Luke 9:62 in his diary: "Jesus said to him, 'No one, after putting his hand to the plow and looking back, is fit for the kingdom of God'" (NASB). This verse challenged Gien and gave purpose and direction to her life. Using this Scripture as a basis, she found it easier to face difficulties, cancel her own desires, and want God's will only.

She met Dawson Trotman, founder of The Navigators, in 1948 in Doorn, Holland. She started the Navigator ministry there by translating The Navigators' *Topical Memory System* into Dutch and handling all the enrollments. Over the years she worked in many capacities with The Navigators. Women who have been personally helped by Gien Karssen can be found on almost every continent of the globe.

Gien was a popular speaker, Bible study leader, and trainer, as well as a freelance writer for Christian periodicals in Europe. The original edition of *Her Name Is Woman* (Book 1) was her first book and the first book ever published by NavPress. She also wrote *Beside Still Waters* and *The Man Who Was Different*.

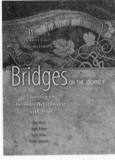

Become the Woman God Created You to Be.

Becoming a Woman of Simplicity
978-1-60006-663-4 | DVD 978-1-61521-821-9

What does it mean to enter into God's rest? Can women today do that, with multitasking, constant communication, and others clamoring for attention? Bestselling author Cynthia Heald helps you quiet the chaos and find true rest for your soul.

Becoming a Woman of Grace
978-1-61521-022-0

This inspirational study guides you on a life-transforming journey into the boundless riches of God's grace. You will explore the many ways in which God's grace enriches your Christian walk and discover how to know His grace more fully.

Becoming a Woman Who Loves
978-1-61521-023-7

In *Becoming a Woman Who Loves*, you'll explore the incredible nature of Christlike love and how God empowers us to love as Jesus loved.

Becoming a Woman of Faith
978-1-61521-021-3

This book will strengthen and encourage you as Cynthia shares candidly from her own faith journey. You'll see yourself in her personal struggles to walk in faith and trust, and you'll learn and grow from her special insights from God's Word.

Becoming a Woman of Strength
978-1-61521-620-8 | DVD 978-1-61747-902-1

We constantly encounter struggles and hardships of all kinds in our lives, but we can respond to them in our own weakness or with God's strength. This Bible study will encourage you to depend upon the strength of the Lord by seeking, waiting, serving, praying, and persevering in Him.

Becoming a Woman of Excellence
978-1-57683-832-7

Society beckons us to succeed—to achieve excellence in our appearance, our earning power, our family life. God Himself also beckons us to be women of excellence. But what exactly is He asking? In this motivational Bible study, you will discover what you should be striving for as you look to God's excellence as a model.

Becoming a Woman of Freedom
978-1-57683-829-7

Is your Christian life weighing you down? Get your second wind to identify and lay aside those burdens that make you feel "stuck." With challenging insights and thought-provoking quotations from classic thinkers and writers, *Becoming a Woman of Freedom* will help you develop the actions and attitudes you need to finish the race with strength.

Becoming a Woman of Prayer
978-1-57683-830-3

In *Becoming a Woman of Prayer*, you will be encouraged to respond to God's invitation to deeper intimacy with Him. Prayer is an opportunity for us to respond to His invitation to intimacy by calling, crying, and singing to Him. This guide shows us how to become women of prayer.

Becoming a Woman of Purpose
978-1-57683-831-0

As you grow toward genuine peace and fulfillment, you'll learn the joy of loving God and others, waiting on Him with hope, trusting Him through suffering, serving Him with reverent fear, and fulfilling His purposes.

Becoming a Woman Whose God Is Enough
978-1-61291-634-7

God desires to bless you with His fullness and to teach you to depend on Him completely. Learn to turn from worldly satisfactions to a life of contentment, from selfishness to humility, and from unbelief to rich fellowship with God.

Available wherever books are sold.

A NavPress resource published in alliance with Tyndale House Publishers, Inc.   CP0795

Women of the Bible You Can Relate To

Believers

Jochebed
Hannah
Rahab
The Jewish Maid
Ruth
Mary

Elizabeth
Anna
The Poor Widow
Mary of Jerusalem
Tabitha
Lois and Eunice

Leaders

Miriam
Deborah
Abigail
The Queen of Sheba
Huldah
The Shunammite

Esther
Mary of Bethany
Mary Magdalene
Lydia
Priscilla
Phoebe

Learners

Eve
Sarah
Rebekah
Leah
Dinah
Tamar

Naomi
Bathsheba
The Widow of Zarephath
Martha of Bethany
The Samaritan Woman
Salome

Wanderers

Hagar
Lot's Wife
Rachel
Potiphar's Wife
Delilah
Peninnah

Job's Wife
Orpah
Michal
Jezebel
Herodias
Sapphira

Gien Karssen's vivid storytelling and deep insights will immerse you in the lives of these women. As you grapple with God's role in each woman's life, you will be inspired to live your own life wholeheartedly for God.

The Her Name Is Woman series is a favorite guide for Bible studies and small groups, with relevant Scripture passages and Bible study questions.

Available everywhere books are sold or online at NavPress.com.
1-855-277-9400

CP0927

Believers: lessons from women of powerful faith explores the lives of Hannah, Ruth, Mary, and nine other women from the Bible who believed God, no matter what. Each of these women held on to God as He took them down a unique path—just as He is doing for you.

Through Gien Karssen's vivid storytelling and deep insights, the lives of these biblical women will instruct and inspire you to embrace a more vibrant faith in your own life. The stories will remind you of people you know, and maybe even of yourself.

Each book in the Her Name Is Woman series brings to life women who are featured in the pages of the Bible. As you grapple with God's role in each woman's life, you will be motivated to live your own life wholeheartedly for God. Each chapter includes relevant Scripture passages and study questions that have made the Her Name Is Woman series a favorite guide for Bible studies and small groups.

GIEN KARSSEN is author of the Her Name Is Woman series. She was married for only six weeks when her husband was interned in a concentration camp during the Nazi Holocaust, where he died. She lived the rest of days avidly mentoring women as part of The Navigators in Europe.

ISBN 978-1-63146-424
Bible Study/Wome
US $9.9

NAVPRESS

A NavPress resource published in alliance with Tyndale House Publishers, Inc.

9 781631 464249   EAN

50999

RASPBERRIES!
An American Tale of Cooperation

By Mary Newell DePalma
Illustrated By Leo Acadia

Mary Newell DePalma wrote this original tale
especially for Teaching Tolerance's Rhinos and Raspberries.

Mary Newell DePalma's illustrations have appeared in newspapers, books and
magazines. She is the author of A Grand Old Tree, the author and illustrator of
The Strange Egg, and the illustrator of numerous other children's books. She lives in
Boston with her husband and their two children. Visit www.marynewelldepalma.com.

Leo Acadia is a fake!... Actually, John S. Dykes markets his digital creations under the
name Leo Acadia (the styles are very different). Leo has been recognized with awards from
The Society of Illustrators, Communication Arts, and American Illustration. They both work
out of the same studio in Sudbury, Massachusetts, but are rarely seen in the same place
at the same time...Hmmmmm. Visit www.leoacadia.com and www.jsdykes.com.